WISDOM *from the*
MIDDLE AGES
for MIDDLE-AGED
WOMEN

Lisa B. Hamilton

MOREHOUSE PUBLISHING
An imprint of Church Publishing Incorporated
HARRISBURG · NEW YORK

Morehouse Publishing, 4775 Linglestown Road, Harrisburg, PA 17105

Morehouse Publishing, 445 Fifth Avenue, New York, NY 10016

Morehouse Publishing is an imprint of Church Publishing Incorporated.

Cover art: "Hildegard von Bingen" by Robin White, Wild Graces, www.wildgraces.com.

Cover design: Brenda Klinger

Interior design by Irene Zevgolis

Library of Congress Cataloging-in-Publication Data
Hamilton, Lisa Belcher, 1959-
   Wisdom from the middle ages for middle-aged women / Lisa B. Hamilton.
     p. cm.
   Includes bibliographical references.
   ISBN 978-0-8192-2237-4 (pbk.)
   1. Middle-aged women—Religious life. 2. Women mystics. 3. Christian women—Religious life. I. Title.
   BV4579.5.H36 2007
   248.8'43--dc22
                                        2007025241

Printed in the United States of America

07 08 09 10 11 12   10 9 8 7 6 5 4 3 2 1

FOR J

"For now the winter is past,
the rain is over and gone"

Song of Solomon 2:11

CONTENTS

APPRECIATIONS

As I've grown in my appreciation for our mystics, I've come to think of these remarkable medieval women as midwives to modern wisdom. Though they died centuries ago, their legacy of wisdom is a living presence that invites me to a deeper vitality. As do those of you who have served as midwives to this book.

First, I thank my son, Ted. Your deepening wisdom only deepens my love for you. What a joy to witness your journey to maturity.

I also thank those who shared their gifts in bringing this idea to publication, especially Nancy Fitzgerald of Morehouse for her talent and skills; Dr. Mary Hope Griffin, for her scholarship; Dianne Defonce of Borders of Fairfield, Connecticut, for her prayerful encouragement; the Sisters of the Circle of St. Peter's Episcopal Cathedral, St. Petersburg, Florida, for their insights; Wendy Shaw for her "Britishness," and the vestry of St. John's Episcopal Church, West Hartford, Connecticut, for inviting me to lead a retreat on English mystics, preventing me from continuing to avoid Margery Kempe.

And I thank my friends, whose loving wisdom inspires me,

especially the Rev. Sarah Buxton-Smith, Cynthia Canaday, Anne and Dr. Bill Coyle, Dr. Shannon Craigo-Snell, the Rev. Loren Gregory, Julie and Jeff Korzenik, Kay Langan, Marilynn Mundy, Inge Osborne, Diane Reed, Joanne Rogers, Victoria Sherrow, the Rev. Dr. Vicki Sirota, and Tory Slosson.

Finally, I thank my fiancé, Jim Grubbs, who can now add to the list of ways in which he blesses me helping bring this book to life every day since its conception.

INTRODUCTION

What *Are* Medieval Mystics Anyway—and
What Difference Do They Make to a Midlife Woman Like Me?

When I wrote letters to Santa, there were two givens. First, I'd forget to keep my crayons out of Trixie's reach, so the waddling mutt would manage to Hoover at least a few. Second, I'd *never* get the first item on the list—the really big present, the thing I couldn't sleep for wanting. Some little girls ask for ponies every December (and are similarly disappointed), but BIG SISTER was always at the top of my list. My brothers were seven and twelve when I was born, and I longed for someone who would help me navigate their teasing and who ranked the importance of a closed toilet seat as highly as I did—someone who understood what it was like to be a *girl*. The big sister I wanted would be the type who wouldn't laugh when I got a really bad haircut the day before school pictures. Instead, she would have just come across a way to fix everything with undetectable bobby pins and judicious combing as recommended in her latest issue of *Glamour*. My big sister would be the kind of big sister who would bring me along to her slumber parties so I wouldn't feel left out.

Although I spent years scoping out my friends' sisters so

I could ask to be adopted, I never did find anyone who fit the bill. The fact is, I pined for the kind of big sister who doesn't really exist. When I saw my friend and her sister pulling each other's hair as they fought over which half of their room was whose, I realized the sad truth—that, like everyone else, sisters are imperfect, even if I didn't want to believe it.

In the end, I found my big sisters after all, though it turns out they lived in a totally different time and place—the Europe of the Middle Ages. Sigmund Freud would probably say that I'm projecting my desire for an all-wise, always welcoming older sister, but my at-long-last adopted sisters are—almost—everything I've always wanted. They're not much help with makeup and hair (medieval recipes for conditioner usually include bear fat and bacon grease), but across the centuries they offer very wise advice about menopause and empty nests and widowhood and divorce and remarriage and retirement planning and self-esteem and this feeling that you'd better live well because there may not be much time left to do so and a whole lot of other issues that are familiar to women my age. All the important stuff.

So why aren't we middle-aged women familiar with these wise and available older sisters? Part of the problem, of course, is that women were often ignored or otherwise written out of history. If you study history in terms of wars and policies, well, those were boys' arenas. But here's another part of the reason we don't hear much about medieval women mystics: we've convinced ourselves we don't want to know.

It's sort of like when I was in college and convinced myself I didn't want to know about sororities. On my first visit to the campus, I didn't even know the meaning of "Greek system." When the admissions interviewer asked, "What would you say if I told you the campus is 90 percent Greek?" I answered, in my best attempt to demonstrate my intellectual prowess, "That's sur-

prising—I mean, you just said most of the students are from the
Midwest, and I didn't know there were that many people of
Greek descent living in this area of the country." What the
admissions counselor meant was that the vast majority of
students lived in fraternity or sorority houses, most of which
looked like country clubs—which was appropriate, because you
had to be a member to live there. This thriving Greek system
meant there were also some leftovers: the Geeks.

I was a Geek. My parents said they couldn't afford for me to
live in a sorority house, and I thought a coed dorm sounded like
more fun anyway. The decision not to "rush"—the process of
induction into a sorority—taught me, a white bread, middle-
class girl from southern Indiana, how it feels to be an outsider.
When I'd naively ask about the intricacies of Greek life ("How
do you get invited to a Kiss-in?" "Does getting pinned hurt?"),
the answer, through perfectly straight teeth and a smirk, was
always, "That's a 'seeky-mysty'"—a mystery I could seek but was
never allowed to understand. So, soon I started convincing
myself that I didn't even care to know.

Which is how it is with the mystics. We define them as
people who achieve oneness with God, or maybe call them
"ambassadors of God," and then we quickly change the subject.
We've convinced ourselves that only dusty old professors and
(even worse) clergy who probably chant psalms in Latin in their
sleep would want to know anything about them. Furthermore,
we've convinced ourselves that mystics are out of our moral
reach—which has given them a bad name. That mystics would
never have dipped into their children's Halloween candy
(of course, mystics wouldn't have had children, because they
certainly wouldn't have had sex!). That mystics would never have
been jealous of someone's perfect home or shiny new car. That
mystics never said the wrong thing at just the right time to spoil
an evening. That they wouldn't know the meaning of "screwed

up," "second-guess," "overdrawn," "overweight." Mystics have a bad wrap, all right, but worst of all, mystics have gotten the reputation for being boring, which serves them right for being so all-fired perfect, and sometimes going on to be sainted, or over-the-top weird.

That's what I thought. Until a church asked me to lead a retreat on English mystics, asking me specifically to include Margery Kempe (c. 1373–after 1438). I skimmed over Margery in divinity school, retaining only that *The Book of Margery Kempe* is usually considered the first autobiography in English, and that she was a sort of medieval desperate housewife. Margery had a bad case of postpartum depression, got religion, and ended up crying so frequently and so hyserically that when she went on pilgrimage, her companions ditched her. Now all of this is roughly true, but when I was forced to read her book, it turned out to be a gift. Margery, I decided, was no crazier than I am. After all, my pain and my expression of it certainly cost me many a friend. More about Margery later, but suffice it to say, once you get to know her, you may think I'm in pretty good company.

No wonder we don't know anything about mystics—with a reputation like theirs, who'd *want* to know them? Ursula King, professor at England's University of Bristol, defines a mystic as "a person who is deeply aware of the powerful presence of the divine Spirit: someone who seeks, above all, the knowledge and love of God and who experiences to an extraordinary degree the profoundly personal encounter with the energy of divine life."[1] But doesn't that describe all of us in our better moments? Maybe we don't seek the knowledge and love of God above *all* else—at least not very often—and maybe our encounters with the divine Spirit aren't always extraordinary. But aren't they always mean-ingful? Think of a mystic this way: simply as a person who's more focused on seeking God than most of us are most of the time, and whose encounters with God are perhaps more dramatic than our own. And she's willing to share, and she probably has a lot to teach us. Which doesn't sound so intimidating.

TIME-TESTED WISDOM

Think of each mystic we'll meet in this book as a big sister who knows a lot about God and about living, and who wants to make sure you never feel alone as she helps you get through life as best you can. Chances are, even if you have sisters, and even if you no longer engage in hair-pulling fights, you could still use someone like that. Besides, one of the best things about becoming middle-aged is that we're finally smart enough to take help anywhere we can find it.

I'm unsure how I came to be middle-aged, but here I am, a plump, hot-flashing cheese in the sandwich of mothering both an aging child and an aging mother, with a side of worries over work and retirement and a large order of friendship and love. If someone (even my imaginary big sister) had told me when I was in my twenties that I'd know so little all these decades later, I would never have believed her. But these days, I've decided that as long as we're living, we're works in progress, and that we're never completely sure about most things.

Maybe it's not menopause that makes so many of us feel disoriented, but the fact that lack of certainty and layers of complications collude in midlife. I once figured out I'd passed the airport in Hartford, Connecticut, when I saw the WELCOME TO RHODE ISLAND sign. I'd probably missed my exit by looking at my map so often—and my mind was more on the conversation my son and I were having between the ringing of our cell phones.

Despite the complexity that marks my midlife, there *are* a few things I am sure of. I love my child more than breathing, though how he came to be taller than I am is, well, beyond me. I was widowed way too young, though my husband's cancer grew us old together. (We were thirty-two when he died.) My mother's advanced Alzheimer's re-teaches me that compassionate nurses are living saints. I love traveling and beaches and New York City, maybe because I'm from a landlocked small town. And I love my fiancé, love him happily and fiercely and forever (yes, love *can* come again, even if it's sixteen years between husbands). A favorite way to relax is to bake bread and pies and cookies and cakes—though watching many of my attempts is apparently more entertaining than eating my creations (my son's response to my reputation as a good cook in my fiancé's family: "That's weird"). I give away as much of the edible stuff as I can, but there's enough left over to leave me struggling with my weight. So I start most days huffing through a thirty-minute session at one of those women-only gyms. Recently, I've added biking or snowshoeing, depending on the weather. All that sweat is also good for my mood. I'm what they call a sexual abuse survivor, though some days I'm not sure what they mean by "surviving," and other days I thrive. My checkered career (the most fun kind of career to have, though the "excitement" that occurs in my checkbook as a result sometimes makes boredom look attractive) includes dabbling into the worlds of public radio, college admissions, refugee resettlement, speechwriting, teaching, television and video-making, publishing—and the priesthood in the Episcopal Church.

Although I take the priesthood and my ministry seriously, I am not overly pious. It often takes me a long time to locate something in the Bible. I don't pray regularly enough or selflessly enough. I know the second verses of very few hymns (maybe none). I've been known to ask God to smite difficult parishioners with a nap when I'm on the way to their hospital rooms. I prefer reruns of *The Simpsons* to vestry meetings. Hence, the dubious introduction by a pal who once tried to get me a boyfriend: "I told him you're a priest, but that you'd never know it." I'm not sure if that was a compliment, but the ensuing relationship never progressed beyond a casual cup of coffee.

My relationship with several mystical types from the Middle Ages has been more enduring. For instance, if my date had taken the time to know me better, he might have learned that I have a theory about parents: we either have the tendency to jump in or to butt out. The trick is figuring out which one you tend to be (of course, this can vary from day to day or situation to situation), which helps you know which direction to take. I confess that I tend to be a jumper-inner rather than a butter-outer. Which is why Julian of Norwich, England, is such a good friend for me to have. Although nobody knows much about Julian's life (we think she died around 1314), she seems to have known a great deal about mothering. She referred to Jesus as "our kind Mother, our gracious Mother," and then wrote about Jesus as the perfect mother, in part because he allows us to make mistakes that allow us to grow up—a good reminder for mothers who tend to jump in too quickly, like me.

God told Catherine of Siena, Italy (1347–1380), that Jesus' divinity is kneaded into the clay of our humanity like one bread, which makes me think Catherine savored the smell of yeast and the silky feel of flour under the heel of her hand, as I do. Teresa of Avila, Spain (1515–1582), certainly knew her way around a kitchen—she once experienced an ecstatic vision while frying eggs. "God is not only found on your knees before the altar," she counseled, "but in the kitchen, among the pots and pans."

Although the mystics may have a lot to tell us about *our* lives, you can see how they might be stumped at a cocktail party by the inevitable question, "What do you *do*?" While Catherine of Genoa, Italy (1447–1510), apparently a financial wiz, could hold forth on her job as the administrator of a huge city hospital (she could also go into what it's like to be trapped in a bad marriage), and musician Hildegard of Bingen, Germany (1098–1179), could enlighten even the tone-deaf on the trials of composing, I suspect the real answer each of these women would want to give would have something to do with what it's like to experience the divine in the here and now in a deeply personal way.

EXPERIENCING THE DIVINE

Experiencing the divine in a deeply personal way is a hallmark of mystics, no matter when they live or what they believe about God. Rabi'a al-'Adawiyya (c. 717–801), who lived in what is now Iraq, was a Sufi Muslim, a sect known for its emphasis on both mysticism and a personal relationship with God. Rabi'a is among the first in a long line of women Sufimystics. Unfraid to bare her soul to God, she implored, "Take my prayer as it is, devil and all." Rabi'a insisted that the path to God is always available and does not require ritual. She asked those who seemed too wrapped up in religious rites, "How long will you keep pounding on an open door?"

Perhaps because mystical experiences are so intensely personal, it's never easy to describe them. Angela of Foligno, Italy (c. 1248–1309), wrote, "I felt it, that God was embracing my soul. I truly did feel that this was happening. But now it seems that everything we are trying to say about this experience reduces it to a mere trifle, because what took place is so different from what can be said about it. I myself am very ashamed that I cannot find better words to describe it." Catherine of Genoa (1447–1510) confessed, "I am more confused than satisfied with the words I have used to express myself, but I have found nothing better for what I have felt."

My friend Sharon sent me what she calls "finger gabbing" the other day. Her wisdom is honed by surviving breast cancer and bicycling cross-country at age sixty-five with a group called Young at Heart. Sharon describes mystical experiences as "common experiences experienced in an uncommon way." Even a flat tire on the cross-country journey gave way to what Sharon considers a mystical experience. She wrote:

> *Somewhere in the Arizona nowhere between Salome and Wickenburg, I was aware of an immense stretch of yellow wildflowers beside me on the roadway. I realized I was thinking of my dad, who passed away some 30 years ago, and especially his letting me help him fix my bicycle. About six months after V.J. Day, he somehow scraped together the money to buy me a bike—a blue Schwinn—for my birthday. What a grand chat we had, tears flowing freely as I rode along the highway. Then the dense stretch of yellow flowers ceased, and I had my first flat tire of the trip, which a friend in our group helped me fix. I told him about my conversation with Dad, and by the time we arrived at our motel, we were singing, "Oh when the saints come biking in, Oh when the saints come biking in, Oh Lord, I want to be in that number, when the saints come biking in." And it finally dawned on me. I was experiencing various forms of immortality in unique ways. It was mystical indeed.*

I love Sharon's description of what is sometimes called a "unitive state" with what lies beyond the everydayness of daily life. Catherine of Genoa described her experience of God as "so submerged in His immense love that I seem as though immersed in the sea, and nowhere able to touch, see or feel aught but water."[2] Catherine of Siena resorts to fire instead of water to describe the indescribable experience of God: "But as a flame burns higher the more fuel is fed it, the fire in this soul grew so great that her body could not have contained it. She could not, in fact, have survived had she not been encircled by the strength of him who is strength itself."[3] Julian wrote about God calling us to union as God's knitting and "oneing" us to himself (or herself, if you prefer).[4] Hildegard described a vision as beyond words, "like a trembling flame, or like a cloud stirred by the clear air."[5]

No matter how slippery a mystical experience becomes when trying to describe it to others, mystics soldier on, sustained by their conviction that the inner life is powerful and important. And this conviction appeals to us, I think. Listen to yourself on the phone with a friend, or in a therapist's office, or e-mailing in the middle of the night. I'll bet phrases like "inner peace," or "feeling grounded" or "needing a center of gravity" or "spiritual health" pop up. Some believe we middle-aged women hunger for such peace, grounding, gravity, or health because we are chronically needed.[6] I think it's at least in part because we've grown up pushing aside, or ignoring, or belittling our inner lives. We've been advised to pattern our lives in ways that can be seen from the outside: careers, money, lovers, and children. But until we tend to our inner lives, nothing on the outside will have any meaning.

Seven hundred years ago, Catherine of Siena, one smart cookie though she had no formal education, understood this longing when she described her "inner cell"—a quiet place with room for only God and the soul, where the soul gathers strength. Although our sister mystics vary widely in terms of personality, place, accomplishments, and life experience, each insisted on room for God—and for herself. Not one found it easy. And not one sugarcoated her struggles. Sometimes they even whined about them. After an extended period of being tormented by demons, Catherine of Siena moaned to Jesus, "And where were *you* when all that was happening?"[7] Angela bluntly complained, "Of what use are revelations, visions, feelings of God's presence?" Mystics are a diverse bunch, but none of them blows smoke, if you know what I mean—not even when they're trying to describe their mystical triumphs of feeling at one with God.

MYSTICAL ROCK STARS

In their day, mystics were celebrities. Granted, word didn't travel fast, but word *did* travel eventually—traveling friars, peddlers, and sailors saw to that. Celebrity magazine cover stories wouldn't have been on who dressed best, but on who prayed best. Blogs would brim with what gets relegated to the weekly "Religion" page in local papers these days. God was the international, national, and local news in those days. Medievals didn't avoid discussing religion; they were more likely to bring up theology before mentioning the weather, since, like everything else, the weather was strictly God's domain.

In our own time, Dylan Thomas came up with a water lily as a metaphor for the mystical ways of God. He wrote a poem entitled "The Force That Through the Green Fuse Drives the Flower."[8] The whole idea of something as elegantly beautiful as a water lily wallowing in mud and yet somehow rising through mud and pond scum toward the light captures for me the way God grows each of us.

MODERN MYSTICAL MOMENTS

Once you look at it through Dylan Thomas's lens—or Julian's or Sharon's or Catherine's, or maybe even your own—you start to see mystical moments all the time. A friend of mine once claimed he knew without doubt that God exists and loves after nearly losing his young son, slippery with sunscreen, to an undertow. Deep awareness of God's love for you can happen when you feel a child's heart beating against your own, or when you knit, or when you fry eggs, or when you fix a flat bike tire.

I think something that happened in my own messy kitchen is mystical. Only now, in middle age, am I discovering my inner Martha Stewart. A few summers ago, my kitchen began to smell like peach cobblers and blueberry pancakes and raspberry jam and red velvet cakes when I—shunner of the sifter, foresaker of the electric mixer—took up baking! The surprise culinary trend continues, and I'm now asking relatives if they happen to have my mother's recipe for lemon meringue pie. Baking, the very activity I ignored so well by practicing the piano as my mother made pies while gamely reeling off secrets of flaky crusts (one tip: use ice water), is somehow helping me come to terms with her as she lives in late-stage Alzheimer's, a disease a friend says we can hope is better on the inside than it looks on the outside. As I cream together the butter and sugar, as I knead the dough, I'm healed by memory. Remembering my mother by taking pleasure in one of her pleasures somehow helps me know her more clearly, unclouded by the longings of who I wanted her to be. I only wish I could have felt this forgiveness, this admiration, this understanding, this acceptance of my mother (and maybe of myself, too) before our roles reversed.

Experiencing the best parts of my mother through engaging in one of the things she did best gives me a sense of how God's love transforms the pain of everyday living, the mistakes we make, the what-ifs and if-onlys. And the wishing, the yearning, gives me a glimpse of how God longs to be known. All of which is even more mystical than the way yeast rolls smell when they're baking.

Maybe we Christians shouldn't be surprised that our lives are as suffused by mystical moments as our dryer traps are full of lint when kids bring their laundry home. Christianity has been mystical from the get-go. What adjective other than "mystical" could you give to a faith that is distinguished by the belief that God was made flesh in the person of Jesus—in the wondrous union of God and humanity in the birth of a helpless infant? When Jesus grew up, he said, "The Father and I are one" (John 22:30), which theologians label "incarnation," but which I call a mystical statement if I've ever heard one. And here's another mystical statement from Jesus: "Inherit the kingdom prepared for you from the foundation of the world; for I was hungry and you gave me food, I was thirsty and you gave me something to drink, I was a stranger and you welcomed me, I was naked and you gave me clothing, I was sick and you took care of me, I was in prison and you visited me" (Matthew 25:31–46). Care for the vulnerable, Jesus said, and you're caring for me—for Jesus resides in each of us. Mystical.

No wonder so many Christians, including our mystics, have strived for union with Christ. Paul seems to have achieved this union; he writes to the Galatians, "it is no longer I who live, but it is Christ who lives in me" (Galatians 2:20). This union seems to have shifted everything for Catherine of Genoa, who reported, "I see without eyes, hear without understanding, feel without feeling, and taste without tasting. . . . Nor can I any longer say, 'My God, my All.' Everything is mine, for all that is God's seems to be wholly mine. Neither on heaven nor on earth shall I ever again use such words, for I am mute and lost in God."[9] If, like most of us, you're not quite in the league of Paul and Catherine of Genoa, take heart. Catherine of Siena said Jesus promises this: "I never give up trying to make you like me so far as you are able to respond."[10]

Catherine of Siena described God as "mad with love and drunk with love." God loves us so madly, with such inebriation and so impartially, that each and every one of is drenched in God's love, no matter what. Whether you're a Sunday school superintendent, a "C & E" (clergyspeak for those who attend church on Christmas and Easter only), an atheist, or an agnostic, God loves you wholly, completely, and eternally. Hildegard referred to God's love as "the Voice of Living Light." And we cannot escape it.

With divine love creating us and lighting our way, our job is to be willing water lilies, as God's love propels us through the green fuse of life. I believe the mystics can help us spend less time burrowing in the mud and more time shooting for the light where we bloom into the creations God intended. This blooming business isn't easy, as we know. The mystics knew that too, and that's why they have so much help to offer us along the way.

A Prayer to Get Started

God of all people, of all times and all places, who made each of us as different as you make the snowflakes, thank you for revealing yourself so differently to each of us. Thank you for honoring our individuality. Thank you for our imaginations that help us describe you. Forgive us when we refuse to acknowledge you. Forgive us for refusing to be open to people and ideas that can teach us about ourselves, our world, and you. Forgive us for shutting out mystical moments. Give us the peace within ourselves to experience you in all the ways you reveal yourself. In praise of you, whom Julian teaches us knits us to yourself, Amen.

Questions for Journaling and Reflection

1. Our mystics present us with a variety of ways to imagine God: a knitter, a kneader, a flame, a cloud, the ocean. What kinds of images come to your mind when you think about God? Why? Have the images changed throughout your life? List the ways you remember imagining God as a child and the ways you imagine God now. Revisit your list from time to time. Notice any patterns?
2. When I dismissed a group of people (the "Greeks" at my college) as unworthy of my time, it was out of jealousy. What about you? Is there anyone or anything you're keeping yourself from learning about?
3. The Bible is brimming with mystical experiences. Which ones resonate with you? Here's a list to get you started: Paul's in Galatians 2:20, Acts 6:9 and 22:7; Peter's in Acts 10:34; Abraham's in Genesis 15; Isaiah's in Isaiah 6;

Ezekiel's in Ezekiel 37 and 40; Daniel's in Daniel 8; Zechariah's in Luke 1; John's throughout the book of Revelation; and Peter, James, and John's experience of Jesus' transfiguration in Matthew 17:1–9.

4. Have you ever had a mystical experience? What was it like? Why do you think you had the experience at exactly that time in your life? Did you share it? What do you think God wants you to do with the experience(s)?

1

I Think I Hear Middle Age Knocking—Should I Get the Door?

It's much easier to date the Middle Ages than to date middle age, as they're attached to a huge time span: the fifth through the fifteenth centuries. This thousand-year span covers a lot of ground: the fall of the Roman Empire; the rise of the monarchy; the Crusades; Viking raids; new trade routes bringing inventions from the East, from silk to gunpowder to compasses; feudalism; the division of Christianity into Orthodox and Roman Catholic churches; illuminated manuscripts; the Black Death; the Hundred Years War; the establishment of universities—all the way up to Martin Luther and the Protestant Reformation.

Historians call them the "Middle" Ages because European history used to be divided into three periods of time: Classical (think Greek and Roman empires), Middle, and Modern (ignited by the invention of the printing press). Think of the Middle Ages as the sandwich generation of history. No wonder the period has something to say to those of us in the midst of midlife. Yet, by and large, the Middle Ages had little that was good to say about women in midlife. In medieval times, women were described with terms like "defiled," "polluted," "tainted," "fickle," "unstable," and "liable to sexual excess." When medieval theologians read the book of Genesis, they concluded that if only Eve hadn't eaten that apple, things would still be as idyllic as they were in Eden and we'd still be perfectly happy all the time.[1] As during antiquity, in the Middle Ages, Eve—and her daughters—were associated with the fleshy, mortal, bodily side of human beings, while Adam—and all men thereafter—were associated with the intellectual and spiritual (and better) part of our nature. (That's what we get for having things like periods and babies.)

Medieval men were heirs to an intriguing theory about women from the Greeks, who viewed us as deformed versions of men. They associated the intellect and the soul with warmth and dryness, while women were linked to the cold and wet. All this played into the theory of "humors" that undergirded medical knowledge, at least through the Middle Ages. When women were menstruating, they were considered especially cold, wet— and dangerous. Even at menopause, women were considered keepers of the coldest, wettest, most corrupt parts of human nature. With a reputation like that, who'd want to spend any time with us? Well, the devil, of course—after all, hadn't he found Eve approachable? Accused of snuggling with Satan, no wonder so many middle-aged medieval women (and even seventeenth-century American women) were blamed for disasters like failed crops, curdled milk, bad weather, and well water gone bad. Perhaps it's no wonder that even modern mothers tend to get blamed for so much.

WHEN DOES MIDLIFE BEGIN?

Though historians have dated the Middle Ages, dating the onset of middle age is a slippery business. Is middle age a number, a set of circumstances, or a state of mind? Is it a question of *when* middle age is, or *what* middle age is? Can we define middle age as the time between attaining adulthood and reaching old age, or between financial independence and the inability to write our own checks? Does middle age begin when you cope with your kids' pimples instead of your own, or when your kids are out of the house? Does middle age begin tidily, with a birthday that ends in zero? And if it does, which one?

It seems to me that middle age tends to catch us by surprise, when we notice that every burner—body, family, relationships, work—is simmering, if not boiling over, all at once. After many a gym conversation on the topic of middle age, I've come to a conclusion. Middle age is when you start hearing your own voice at least as loudly as you hear those of others. As I overheard a gray-headed woman exclaim in a firm voice the other day, "This is the first time in my life I'm not doing what someone else is telling me to do. I'm finally doing what *I'm* telling myself to do." That's as good a definition of middle age as I've heard.

Now that we're living longer,[2] our children's adolescence may stretch further than that of our parents, but it's middle age, with its relative good heath, that's expanded the most. Most of us enjoy many more years of good health than our parents or grandparents. As this period of good health varies widely from person to person, it's no wonder we have a hard time defining middle age. As my friend Carolyn said ruefully, "Middle age is when you wake up in the middle of the night and don't know if it's menopause, or because your mother's living alone, or because your teenager's out with the car."

YOUR INNER MIDLIFE

Both Carolyn and psychiatrist Carl Jung (1875–1961) got me thinking about middle age as something that has less to do with externals—age or menopause or aging parents or an empty nest—and more to do with who we are *internally*. To paraphrase

Jung, in the first several years of life, to survive in the world it's necessary to mostly follow the voices of others: parents and teachers and bosses. Growing up begins when we hear our own voices at least as loudly as we hear those of others. That's *not* to say that we should spend our children's college savings on a sports car—that kind of self-centeredness is adolescent. But it *is* to say that we start growing up when we take our own voices seriously. Some of us embark on this uncharted journey earlier than do others; sadly, some of us never begin. Most of us start hearing whispers of our own voice somewhere in our forties, and a few of us find our voices' volume steadily increasing. But once your own voice has your attention, it's too interesting and too wise and too unique to ignore.

Jung marks the point at which he himself could no longer quiet his own voice when he parted ways with his mentor, Sigmund Freud (1856–1939), after publicly challenging some of the older man's most important theories. Finding his own way wasn't easy, but it propelled Jung into becoming his own person. Jung claimed that in order to grow up, each of us has to allow an immature self to die so that we may become our true self.

For mystery writer Agatha Christie, on the other hand, middle age seemed to be a sort of second wind that breezed in. Christie's fiftieth birthday brought her an explosion of new interests, ideas, and priorities.

Christie's second wind doesn't sound exactly like Jung's step into the unknown, yet, taken together, they describe the fear and excitement that are both part of hearing your own voice calling you to embark on a new beginning. It can be confusing and downright disorienting—and can take you deeper into your spirituality than you ever wanted to go. Even Jung claims that "the search for the authentic self" includes the search for meaningful connection to others, to nature, and to our Creator. So, as you start to hear your own voice more clearly, you may find yourself hearing God's more clearly as well.

MYSTICAL MIDLIFE STIRRINGS

When she was "forty-two and seven months old" (and around the time when women ceased menstruating in her day), a German nun, Hildegard of Bingen, began listening in on herself. She had had visions since shortly after her birth in 1098, and those visions came to her easily. "I had sensed in myself wonderfully the power and mystery of secret and admirable visions from my childhood," she wrote,

> *that is, from the age of five—up to that time, as I do now. This, however, I showed to no one except a few religious persons who were living in the same manner as I; but meanwhile, until the time when God by His grace wished it to be manifested. I concealed it in quiet silence. But the visions I saw I did not perceive in dreams, or sleep, or delirium, or by the eyes of the body, or by the ears of the outer self, or in hidden places; but I received them while awake and seeing with a pure mind and the eyes and ears of the inner self, in open places, as God willed it.*[3]

Hildegard never seemed to doubt her gifts, but she did learn to keep quiet about them. Did her older siblings make fun of her? Did her mother call her a tattletale? Were older women jealous of her visions? We'll never know, but we do know that Hildegard, to be true to herself, began to write down her visions, commanded, it seems, by direct orders from God. She wrote, "When I had passed out of childhood and had reached the age of maturity mentioned above, I heard a voice from Heaven saying, 'I am the Living Light, Who illuminates the darkness. The person I have chosen and whom I have miraculously stricken as I willed, I have placed among great wonders.'"[4]

Still, Hildegard struggled, not so much with the truth of her visions, but with her worthiness to receive them. God continued to nag Hildegard. "And again I heard a voice from Heaven saying to me, 'Cry out therefore and write thus!'" Seven years after God commanded her to write down her visions, Hildegard was agonizing over seeking a publisher. Even nine centuries ago, affirmation from others was sometimes necessary, and so Hildegard wrote Bernard of Clairvaux for advice. The abbot was so impressed that he showed a sample of Hildegard's work to the pope. In 1152, Hildegard published the first of three books, *Scivias* (meaning "know the paths!").

Over the course of the decade Hildegard spent writing *Scivias*, she gained the courage to become a sort of independent contractor who left the security of corporate life. The long-established "double monastery" where Hildegard and her fellow nuns lived was coed, but the authority figures for both monks and nuns were male. At fifty-three, Hildegard left her old monastery and established a monastery for women several miles away, which she governed so effectively that soon there were too many nuns for the original convent to hold. So, at sixty-seven, Hildegard embraced another new beginning when she founded a sister house to handle the overflow.

A cynic might ask here if the overflow was due in part to Hildegard's belief that it was preferable to drink beer rather than water for "rosy cheeks," but in any case, Hildegard is a powerful role model for those of us who long, in *our* middle age, to bring the expertise we've gained working for others to working for ourselves. Thank God Hildegard listened to herself.

Those of us who know how painful it can be to hear ourselves and then to pay attention to ourselves wouldn't wish the difficulty on anyone we love. And yet, I wonder if it's actually possible to hear yourself (or to grow in any significant way) *without* struggle. Angela of Foligno, who lived about two centuries after Hildegard and about seven before us, didn't have an easy time of it, but eventually, she shouted to the world, "This world is pregnant with God!"[5] After much suffering, Angela seemed to hear her own voice with ease. Angela lost her husband, all of her several sons (so far as we know, she had no daughters), and her mother within a year to the Black Death, and regained peace of mind through pilgrimage, prayer, and the visions she received. Eventually, she became a Franciscan tertiary (a layperson who lives by the order's principles) and dictated two books to a relative, Fra Arnaldo, a Franciscan friar. Angela's first book, *Memoriale*, completed in 1296 or 1297, is marked by insecurity. Fra Arnaldo records her every utterance, including her uncertainty of her worthiness and her pitiful hunger for a complete knowledge of God's presence and love.

Somewhere between her first and second books, however, Angela seemed to find her stride. A new and improved Angela authored *Instructiones*, which appeared after her death in 1309. In it, with confidence and firm conviction, she advised Franciscan friars, whom she viewed as her adopted sons, on spirituality. As Dorothy Disse, webmaster of the premiere site on women who've been neglected by history, observes, "What is fascinating is the difference in tone between the voices of the two works: in *Memoriale*, Angela needs to constantly 'feel' the presence of God and is unsure of her ability to make everything clear to the questioning Arnaldo; in *Instructiones*, Angela is sure of herself and her God and believes that she can help her 'sons.'"[6] In the dozen or so years between her books, Angela seems to have passed the threshold into mature middle age, and to have begun not only hearing herself, but God as well.

INCHING TOWARD MATURITY

As a college friend of mine once observed, "We're all only as mature as we have to be." True enough, and because it's also true that it isn't easy to mature, sometimes it helps to have a nudge from a friend. Clare of Assisi, Italy (1193/4–1253), encouraged a follower seeking funding for her monastery to ignore the pope and to listen to her own voice, advising, "Even though you must respect him, do not follow his counsel."[7] In other words, don't try to get by in life without ever hearing the voice of another soul, but respect your own voice, value your own intuition, pay close attention to your own ideas and thoughts and feelings. You have to be willing to become your true self, a major step in becoming a mature human being.

And take heart that the process can usually be counted on to be interesting. Even Agatha Christie, who saw middle age as a time of growth as welcome as an early spring, hit some bumps along the way. She said that when playing the character you've invented for yourself becomes tiresome, you "relapse into individuality," which can be disconcerting for others, but a relief to yourself.[8] I find Christie's image of relapsing into herself especially helpful because it reminds me that I began life as myself—a child of God.

For me, having a child helped me to see myself as a child of love. Several years ago, when I was just beginning to hear my own voice, my then-toddler and I made frequent trips to the Pittsburgh Zoo. If you know Pittsburgh, you know it's a town full of tunnels, including the one at the zoo's entrance. I'd push Teddy's stroller through the tunnel and my voice would echo, "I love you, Teddy." Before long, he'd squeal back, "Love *you*, Mumma." Even then, I knew I would always treasure the memory of our voices bouncing off the granite and carrying us toward a shared adventure. And I always hoped those echoes would stay in my son's heart so that he could hear them whenever he needed to.

A gentle and honest view of themselves characterizes virtually all of our mystics; for instance, Julian claimed, "Our Lord revealed this to me in the completeness of his love, that we are standing in his sight, yes, that he loves us now whilst we are here as well as he will when we are there, before his blessed face."[9] Teresa of Avila reminds us that our souls are valuable, and "must always be considered as plentiful, spacious and large."[10] "All these women," concludes Carol Lee Flinders, writing about seven women mystics in *Enduring Grace*, "display quite a sturdy sense of self."[11] Yet here we sit, in the twenty-first century, when "midlife crisis" is as frequent a topic of conversation as "the terrible twos," and many of us feel anything but sturdy.

Sue Shellenbarger, who writes the "Work & Family" column for the *Wall Street Journal*, says she received more mail when she lampooned her midlife crisis than she did about any column on any other topic. "I had no idea that women got this, too," one man wrote. Shellenbarger found that approximately 38 percent of women and 36 percent of men claim they're undergoing or have undergone a midlife crisis. Although it may not necessarily be a catastrophe, Shellenbarger insists that a midlife crisis cannot be ignored. "People think it's like a grease fire in a frying pan—you put it out and it's over," she says. "What I think is, it's like an earthquake changing the terms of your life."[12] After interviewing fifty women between the ages of thirty-seven and fifty-five for her book, *The Breaking Point: How Female Midlife Crisis Is Transforming Today's Women*, Shellenbarger reports, "I found the ones who tried to repress their midlife crisis to be the most miserable"—and regretful. More commonly, the women Shellenbarger interviewed used their so-called crisis as a catalyst for growth. She observes, "Every one of them who had the courage and resolve to make changes was positive about it. In some ways, maybe this allows women to give themselves permission to change."[13]

I like the idea that something defined as a crisis can also bring permission to grow. But what's the difference between women who soar in midlife and women who curl up and wait for old age? I see women whose divorce ends their vitality as well as their marriages and women for whom the pain of divorce includes wings. I see women who silently implode as their children's lives expand beyond them and women who find freedom in their empty nest. I see women such as Angela, whose suffering increases their ability to love, and women who weather the storms of loss without any discernable signs of growth.

I think the women who listen to themselves are more likely to find midlife a time of renewal. You may find yourself saying some things that are hard to hear. There may be things about your life and yourself that make you miserable, and change won't be easy. You may find yourself facing the reality that it is too late for some things—too late to be a prodigy at anything, too late to have a baby, too late to model bridal gowns. Your dreams may have to shift. You may never be a Broadway sensation, but you can be a star in your community theater group. If you resume piano lessons after a thirty-year hiatus, people probably won't pay to hear you play, but you'll enjoy the sheer pleasure of making music. Recently, I decided to take sketching lessons just because I wanted to try it. The hardest part has been shutting off the tapes of adults from kindergarten on who complained that my art was messy. Well, I'm still a messy person, but I'm loving learning sketching skills, because I simply love doing it. So I'm listening to my inner artist, messy as she is.

LISTENING FOR GOD IN MIDLIFE, THEN AND NOW

The good news is that, if you listen to everything you have to say, painful parts and all, you may also hear yourself, and no doubt your God, encouraging you to grow in ways you never thought possible. Besides, trying to hold back the tide of yourself requires so much energy that it can make you ill, as Hildegard learned. She wrote: "But although I heard and saw these things, because of doubt and low opinion of myself and because of diverse sayings of men, I refused for a long time a call to write, not out of stubbornness but out of humility, until weighed down by a scourge of God, I fell onto a bed of sickness." This "scourge" was a particularly excruciating migraine. Hildegard was brimming with creativity, which she came to call "greening" of the spirit. In addition to the art and words through which she communicated her visions, she composed more than eighty pieces of music, wrote medical, botanical, and geological treatises, and created an alternative alphabet. But when she dammed the flow of her creativity, her blood vessels literally expanded, the migraine headaches, perhaps a sign that her soul was being blocked, was in dire need of release.

We all know the biblical advice, "Be still and know that I am God" (Psalm 46:10), and we all know how difficult that is to do with cell phones ringing and airplanes roaring and quotas to make and children and grandchildren to raise and doctor's appointments to keep. For me, it helps if I light a candle, which brings back memories of Taizé, a Christian community in a tiny French town where I led groups of suburban Connecticut teenagers on weeklong pilgrimages. Worship at Taizé is three times a day, and consists mostly of chanting, silence, and lots of candles. I always chuckled inwardly when the same teenagers I'd had such a hard time quieting long enough to give them their cabin assignments claimed, "My favorite part was the silence." I knew exactly what they meant, because when I light the candle and sit quietly, I seem to hear my own voice best. I suspect the memory of being surrounded by the community the Taizé brothers provide for teenagers from all over the globe has something to do with it. In those quiet times, I offer God my own voice, my own self, and feel grateful that I am the only person in all creation with exactly my voice. I am grateful that God's light within me encourages me to use my voice, which is the truth of me. And I remember that, as God told the mystic Mechthild of Magdeburg, "No one can burn the truth."

A PRAYER TO GET STARTED

God of every season of our lives, of every age, of every time, of every human being: thank you for Hildegard and Julian and Angela and Mechthild, and all the wise women who teach us to listen to ourselves. Thank you for nagging Hildegard to express what she knew of you. Thank you for leading Julian to a life in which she could meditate and share her visions. Thank you for Angela's ability in her suffering to hear and share her voice with confidence. Forgive our doubt and low opinion of ourselves. Give us the patience to listen to others, but grant us the courage to value our own voices. Open our ears to hear all the voices of our lives, yours and ours and those of others. Let us hear your voice and express you in the voice you've given us. In the name of you, whom Hildegard told us is "the Living Light," Amen.

QUESTIONS FOR REFLECTION AND JOURNALING

1. Nell Morton (1905–1987) wrote one of my favorite books, *The Journey Home.* One of her ideas is that we hear one another into speech—that simply knowing that we're listened to enables us to express our deepest thoughts and feelings. What do you think? What role does listening— to others, to God, and to yourself—play in your life? Morton went so far as to imagine God as a giant ear. Borrow Morton's image for a day or so and see (or perhaps hear) what happens.

2. How would you describe yourself at midlife? Are you a grease fire, an earthquake, a pair of eyes silently observing, an overflowing vessel, an echoing tunnel?

3. Draw yourself a pie chart with a "piece" representing

every waking hour of the day. Note what you're hearing from yourself during each of those hours. And what are others hearing you say? How alike or different is what you're hearing and what you're saying? Try this again a week, a month, a season later. How do the charts compare? What do they tell you about yourself?

4. I define middle age as when you start listening to yourself at least as well as you listen to others. How do *you* define middle age? How does this compare with your mother's, or your grandmothers', definition? How do you think today's teenage girls define middle age? And how do you think they'll come to define it when they reach midlife themselves?

2

Putting the Self in Self-Esteem

Have you heard the term "Age Quake"? In the United States alone, there are some 60 million women over the age of forty, and they're six times more likely than their mothers to take or share fiscal responsibility,[1] which makes us midlife women a force to be reckoned with.

On my best days, I feel pretty powerful, and the transition to middle age feels exciting, empowering, and renewing. In fact, many researchers conclude that for women, the fifties in particular is the prime time of life. Or, as folk singer Susan Werner puts it in a song title, "May I Suggest This Is the Best Time of Your Life?"

But the transition to midlife is also complicated—at least according to the National Association of Social Workers (NASW) in a recently released study, "Women at Midlife: Life Experiences and Implications for the Helping Professions." The organization's work draws on 232 American studies covering "family relationships, work, health, psychological well-being, developmental issues, identity, menopause and sexuality."[2]

Among the study's conclusions is that

> *midlife is a time when many women come into their*
> *own, feeling grounded, independent and satisfied with*
> *what they have. In one study cited by the authors, near-*
> *ly half of women age 51 reported that their lives were*
> *'first rate,' and they experienced high levels of personal*
> *achievement and a new sense of adventure as parenting*
> *roles and other duties subsided. In addition, midlife*
> *women with greater ego resiliency—the ability to*
> *flexibly and resourcefully cope with stressors—were more*
> *likely to report life satisfaction, another study found.*

Did you catch that phrase "ego resiliency"? What the NASW
calls "the ability to flexibly and resourcefully cope with stressors"
just means that it's easier to ride the waves of middle age if you
have resources—money, education, friends, health. No wonder
the researchers found that "midlife is the most tumultuous time
of life for low-income African-American women, for example,
and midlife women in ill health may have a particularly tough
time." As we work to right the inequities faced by women of
color, women in poor health, women with little money, and
women with inadequate education, it can be empowering to
remember that our medieval sisters, mystic or not, were no
strangers to struggle.

FINDING YOURSELF IN THE MIDDLE AGES
Medieval society made self-esteem at least as complicated an
issue for our medieval sisters as it is for us. On the one hand, the
rules were harsh, and death was an acceptable punishment. On
the other hand, everyone knew the rules, and if you obeyed them,
you didn't have to go it on your own.

In an atmosphere as precarious as the Middle Ages, rife with oppression and war and disease and loss, it's no wonder the focus was on survival instead of on self, which meant the idea of self-esteem had to wait a while. Anthropologist Joseph Campbell believed the concept of an independent, self-directed "self" didn't start to develop until about eight hundred years ago. Medievals would have thought the idea of "finding yourself" was selfish, while we moderns tend to think that finding ourselves is required to live a fulfilling life. An up side of medieval life was that you could draw on the accumulated wisdom of the community, but the down side was that your individual self could get lost for the sake of tradition. And some would argue that while an up side to modern life is permission to "do it my way," a down side is that drawing on your community's accumulated wisdom is often frowned upon.

Our medieval mystics, who had only heard of "self" in terms of selfishness, valued the self in ways that enhanced their communities. Julian of Norwich, for instance, could be seen as selfish because she chose to live a life of solitude, set apart from her community. But via her cell's window, facing the street, she was constantly "on call" to the people outside. Finding a way to nurture both one's self and one's community is no easy trick in any time, and the fact that these medieval mystics were able to pull it off in *their* time is particularly remarkable. They are "midwives to the soul" indeed.[3]

Catherine of Siena claimed that God told her, "Here is the way, if you would come to perfect knowledge and enjoyment of me, eternal Life: Never leave the knowledge of yourself. Then, put down as you are in the valley of humility you will know me in yourself, and from this knowledge you will draw all that you need."[4] What a relief to be given permission—even to be commanded—to listen to and to know yourself. These words of God via Catherine bear repeating: "Never leave the knowledge of yourself." And because we're human, we need to start knowing

God by knowing ourselves. That makes getting to know the self a humble and unselfish—even a crucial act, if we're to participate fully in this life and to love God completely. Yunus Emre, a thirteenth-century Turkish male mystic, defends the love of self simply: "We love the created for the Creator's sake."[5]

All this is not to suggest that if only you were as wise as a medieval mystic, you'd never struggle to feel good about yourself. Hildegard of Bingen likened herself to "a weak and fragile rib." Clare of Assisi described herself "a useless handmaid and unworthy servant." Julian called herself "a wretched worm" and "a woman, ignorant, weak and frail." Scholar Monica Furlong speculates, "Their insistence suggests that they are suffering, not surprisingly, from a damaged or broken self-esteem and a socially imposed sense of inferiority." While it may well be that our mystics disrespected themselves as a survival strategy—what they had to say was radical enough without making it sound as if they were proud of who they were—it's still "painful to observe women of genius . . . making their ritual obeisance."[6]

JULIAN OF NORWICH: SELF-ESTEEM IS A WORK IN PROGRESS

Julian not only wrote the first book by a woman in English, she wrote the book twice. The first version, or Short Text, was written soon after May 8, 1373, when she received—on what everyone thought was her deathbed—sixteen visions of Christ. The second version, or Long Text, written some twenty years later, is nearly six times longer than the first. Julian omitted those self-deprecating remarks in her second book. Here's how scholar Carol Flinders views this shift:

> *Taken together, the changes Julian made record a fundamental transformation in the author's own perception of herself. Over the two decades following her revelations,*

the astonished visionary evolved gradually into a confident, fully established spiritual teacher. In the Short Text, *she wrote, "God forbid that you should say or assume that I am a teacher, for that is not and never was my intention; for I am woman, ignorant, weak and frail." Twenty years later, she removed this disclaimer, for by then she had accepted her role as spiritual counselor, knowing full well by that time that whatever she might accomplish in that role was not her own doing anyway, but God's.*[7]

By the time she wrote her Long Text, Julian was a sort of drive-through therapist. Soon after receiving the "showings of God's love," as she called them, Julian became what was known as an anchoress, vowing to live enclosed in a cell consisting of a room or two attached to a church. There she dedicated her life to prayer, contemplation, and solitude, and also gave counsel. This wasn't an especially odd way to spend one's life in fourteenth-century Norwich—probably around thirty anchoresses (or their male counterparts, anchorites) were in the city at any given time. Julian was "anchored" at St. Julian's church in Norwich; she took her name from the church—we don't even know her birth name or whether or not Norwich was her hometown.

Although the church was bombed in World War II, it has been rebuilt; today, visitors can pray and reflect where Julian did. In accordance with rules drawn up for anchoresses and anchorites in the thirteenth century, Julian's cell contains three windows—one opening to the church so she could see Mass celebrated, a second to receive food and other necessities, and the third opening onto the street, making Julian a captive audience for anyone who needed a listening ear.

I think having someone to confide in must have been

especially important to Julian's visitors, because it could be risky business if someone learned you questioned accepted religious beliefs in the Middle Ages. Being called a heretic could be a death sentence. For instance, in 1401, Henry IV of England and his bishops passed a statute called "The Necessity of Burning Heretics"—which they considered necessary because the people were being led astray from the church's teachings, and thereby endangering their souls. Perhaps to give heretics a chance to save themselves from hell, there was a sort of warning system: flogging at the cathedral was the normal punishment for first-time offenders, while burning was saved for repeaters. Interestingly, it was civic rather than church officials who punished heretics. So if your punishment was the loss of property (common in northern Italy and southern France), the town benefited. Medieval folks didn't separate church and state, and both church and civic authorities were more likely to appeal to fear than faith in disciplining the masses.

SEEKING THE SELF IN THE SELFLESS

This severe attitude toward religious "seekers," as we might call them, was not confined to England by any means. Catherine of Siena was interrogated by the Dominicans (although, or perhaps especially, because she was a Dominican tertiary—a sort of lay associate) a year after Julian received her visions. She was accused of relying too much on what she discerned as God's will rather than on the church's teachings. Catherine and Julian's Swedish contemporary, Birgitta (1303–1373), faced similar criticism. A widow with eight children, she made a pilgrimage all the way to Rome so she could pray and write. There were probably no objections to her tender visions of the Virgin Mary, who gave Birgitta a firsthand account of the birth and crucifixion of Christ. It was likely claiming that Jesus told her he was unhappy with the church that got her kicked out of the lodgings she'd been given at a cardinal's palace. According to Birgitta, Jesus said, "It is a very long time since the Church of Rome, the highest authority in the world, pleased God by its holiness and its virtuous and exemplary life as it once did."[8] To question the church was to question the very glue that held the community together.

It's hard to overestimate the church's impact on medieval society; it's probably accurate to say that the church *was* medieval society. So, to question the church was radical indeed, though more than a few of our mystics did so. The church was the sole source of education for the entire society, from the few fledgling academics to the illiterate masses. Stories in stained glass filled in for books and medieval drama was the television of its day. Every medieval medium—sermons, stained glass, manuscripts, illuminations, dramas, songs—functioned to teach dogma as well as to entertain. The teaching was not to be disputed, and any disagreements you had were to be kept to yourself.

The church caught on early to the power of "edutainment"— especially through drama. Maybe reenactment came naturally, because the Mass is in many ways a reenactment of Christ's sacrifice. In any case, throughout Europe in the early Middle Ages, clergy enacted stories commemorated by various feast days on cathedral porches. By the late Middle Ages, simple tableaux had evolved into elaborate series of plays dramatizing all of Christianity's major events, from the creation to judgment day. By then, these "mystery plays" were funded by and acted out by members of guilds. In fact, one definition of "mystery" comes from the late Latin word for craft, which of course harkens to the medieval trade guilds. (The guilds had an almost macabre sense of humor when it came to dividing responsibilities. For instance, in fifteenth-century York, the pinners guild, whose members handcrafted pegs, was responsible for the crucifixion play.)

While it's important to take the mystery plays into account when trying to figure out where ordinary people got their ideas about God and self during the Middle Ages, there's a frequently overlooked art form that had great impact on the lives of medieval folks: preaching. For starters, preaching was usually in the language of the people, although the Mass, of course, was sung or said in Latin. So hearers must have felt they were being personally addressed by preaching clergy, who were more powerful than they. And it's just human nature to listen well when we're being paid a compliment. Second, there was the medieval phenomenon of mendicant friars—monks belonging to orders such as the Franciscans, the Carmelites, the Dominicans, and the Augustinians who traveled throughout Europe to spread the gospel. Probably the best known of these mendicants was Francis of Assisi (1182–1226), who became a traveling preacher with encouragement from Clare, from whom he sought advice on the matter. These mendicant friars, dusty from their journeys and dependent on the kindness of strangers, must   have   been the celebrities of their day. They were frequently charismatic, eloquent speakers—and their presence broke up the monotony of daily life. Medieval preachers, whether on a pulpit or in a public square, commanded attention.

The medieval church literally put the fear of God into its donors. For instance, it was widely believed that neglecting to tithe—giving 10 percent of one's earnings to the church—lead to hell. Hell wasn't debatable in the Middle Ages. Each wave of the Black Death was further proof of God's anger and of humanity's sin. Sin wasn't a concept tentatively whispered about during Lent, sin was a reality that took seven forms—pride, greed, extravagance/lust, envy, gluttony, anger, sloth—and was divided into venial, which got you confession, and mortal, which got you hell. No wonder Dante's (1265–1321)

Inferno contained such detailed punishments.

NEW VOICES

Among the newer though no less harsh voices that strove to be heard over the medieval din of fire and brimstone was that of the religious order known as the Lollards. Their story shows how risky it was to be a medieval heretic. The Lollards' roots can be traced to Julian's contemporary, John Wycliffe (c. 1320–1384), who translated the Bible into English and otherwise enraged authorities, and finally had the good fortune to die before they could kill him. The authorities got the last word though, declaring him a "stiff-necked heretic" and burning his books and his bones—twelve years after his death, which shows they weren't afraid to hold a grudge. It also shows how outrageously dangerous the authorities thought the Bible was in the hands of the masses, living or dead. It could lead to people forming heretical opinions, which we might term expressing self-esteem, but which medieval authorities saw as a way to condemn yourself and anyone you might have influenced to eternal damnation.

As if believing that the Bible should be available in the language of the people weren't enough, the Lollards further flaunted established religious beliefs, claiming that pious laypeople were just as worthy as ordained priests to baptize and preach, and denying the church a role in getting people into heaven. Having enough of what we might call a healthy self-esteem in the Middle Ages was dangerous. Self-esteem hadn't been invented, and nothing about it was valued. The church, not the self, was to be a person's inner compass. To question the church must have felt like you were risking not only your earthly life, but your eternal life as well. Yet, our mystics were so certain of God's love that they found the courage to question accepted beliefs. For instance, Julian must have been reminded of how dangerous her beliefs were every time a heretic was burned to death. What was called "Lollards' Pit" was downwind from her cell.

MIDLIFE SELF-ESTEEM, THEN AND NOW

No wonder Julian referred to life as we know it as "our dying living." Given the culture of death that surrounded Julian—heretics burned at the stake, accidents and disease claiming half of all medieval European children before age five, the plague killing about a third of the English population, the risks of childbirth, frequent war, and famine—the wonder is that she was so optimistic and so certain that each individual self is beloved by God. As Dorothy Disse observes, "It is as if Julian saw the need to offer an antidote to the pervasive fear of sin and death and damnation."[9]

Make no mistake, Julian was not worshipping the self. If we want to make peace with ourselves, Julian told us, we need to enter through God, who lovingly encircles us. She placed our selves squarely *within* God, writing,

> *God is nearer to us than our own soul, for he is the ground in which it stands. . . . Our soul reposes in God in its true rest, and stands in God, its true strength, and is fundamentally rooted in God, its eternal love. So if we want to come to know our soul, and enjoy its fellowship as it were, it is necessary to seek it in our Lord God in whom it is enclosed.*[10]

Though separated by place (Italy versus England) and time (nearly a century earlier), Angela of Foligno's report of the divine resonates with Julian's. According to Angela, God told her, "I am deeper within your soul than your soul is to itself."[11] Again, the advice is to know yourself through knowing God.

This advice rings true for me in a very personal way. As is

common for victims of childhood sexual abuse, I grew up taking responsibility for everything that went wrong. The things that were done to me, and the pain they caused, were because I was such a bad little girl that I needed to be punished. The only way I could make sense of my environment was to assume that I had caused it. This very unhealthy magical thinking gave me a way of making sense of the random, the painful, the confusing—and it isn't an unusual coping mechanism. None of this is far from the medieval belief that one's sin caused disease, or that a witch must have been responsible for well water gone bad, or that whatever suffering comes in this life or the next is because we deserve it.

Maybe that's why Julian is such an inspiration for me. Though living in a time when any attempt to love herself was assaulted by harsh realities, a misogynist culture and a church more concerned with human sin than with God's love, she somehow heard God and told her contemporaries and us that we are worth loving. At the edge of death, Julian found Christ. Over time, she found herself and became a gift to the world. Although good therapy and good friends can help immensely, ultimately, only God can love us fully enough to help us stop hating ourselves and begin seeing ourselves as the precious creation each of us is. I wonder if there was an element of self-loathing that brought on Julian's mysterious disease, so powerful that it brought her to the brink of death (as her mother watched, a priest gave Julian last rites), and yet so powerless in the face of Christ's love that it was used for great good.

Julian wrote of her horrifying experience, "It was at this time that our Lord showed me spiritually how much he loves us. I saw that he is everything that we know to be good and helpful. In his love he clothes us, enfolds and embraces us; that tender love completely surrounds us, never to leave us. As I saw it he is everything that is good."[12]

My path toward self-esteem is pockmarked with memories

that trip me and sometimes toss me into an emotional ditch. God's love lights the path, however, and I am sustained by all kinds of blessings—faithful friends, good therapy, an interesting world, a loving fiancé and son—but my job is being patient. Julian has convinced me that God wants me to love myself. In one of her visions, God showed her

> *a little thing, the size of a hazelnut, on the palm of my hand, round like a ball. I looked at it thoughtfully and wondered, "What is it?" And the answer came, "It is all that is made." I marveled that it continued to exist and did not suddenly disintegrate; it was so small. And again my mind supplied the answer, "It exists, both now and for ever, because God loves it." In short everything owes its existence to the love of God.*[13]

If God loves something as common as a hazelnut, God surely loves me. If something as delicate as a hazelnut is sustained, so shall I be. If a simple hazelnut exists because God loves it, so do each of us complicated human beings. I am grateful for the decades of her life Julian gave to living an unadorned life. I think of the patience it must have taken to grow into the secluded and demanding life of an anchoress. I recognize how much healing she must have received from a life that demanded so much patience. And I'm grateful that she shared her wisdom.

I'm also grateful for Fred "Mister" Rogers, creator and host of America's *Mister Rogers' Neighborhood*, who is one of my heroes. If every child knew early on that just being yourself is a gift and was aware of being special, the world would soon be a better reflection of heaven. And I agree with his statement, "The world needs a sense of worth, and it will achieve it only by its people feeling that they are worthwhile."[14] So don't hold back. Self-esteem is a necessary traveling companion on the path to God.

Like the medieval mystics, love yourself as a way of loving your Creator and our world.

A PRAYER TO GET STARTED

God of each of us, who loves us in our faults and struggles and sins, thank you for working so hard to let us know you love us. Thank you for manifesting yourself and your love of each of us in ways that speak so perfectly to each self you have created. Help us to remember that you cherish each of us. Forgive us when we forget. Help those of us drowning in the familiar waters of self-loathing breathe instead the air of self-esteem. And when we are firmly on the shore, help us to rescue others by reminding them of your immense love. In the name of you, whom Julian reminds us is closer than our own breath, Amen.

QUESTIONS FOR JOURNALING AND REFLECTION

1. One of Julian's visions was of Jesus thanking us for being human when we get to heaven. The setting is a feast over which Jesus presides, "the marvelous music of his unending love showing in the beauty of his blessed face." And "the Lord said, 'Thank you for all your suffering, the suffering of your youth.'"[15] What specific things do you think Jesus will thank you for?

2. When historians write about the Middle Ages, they list the reasons it was so hard to thrive: the Black Death, the carnage of the Crusades, frequent famine, and childhood mortality. What do you think future historians will write about our era? What challenges us, and what blesses us, today? What challenges and blesses *you*?

3. Have you ever written or spoken about yourself in a denigrating way, like so many of "our" mystics did? Why? Were you afraid? Were you hoping to attract approval? Did you feel this language was expected of

you? How did you feel afterward?

4. Julian said that we know ourselves only, paradoxically, by knowing God. What or who helps you know yourself? Is it ever painful, and if so, how and why? Keep in mind Julian's hopeful advice: "Yet when we know and see truly and clearly what our self is, than shall we truly and clearly see and know our Lord God in fullness of joy."[16]

3

BODY LANGUAGE AT
MIDLIFE: SAY WHAT?

A very wise eighty-something woman in a parish I once served offered an astute observation about menopause. "Menopause is a breeze if you're happy, but it can really throw women who are unhappy," she told me. "They can talk all they want about hormones and soy, and I don't doubt there's something to all of them. But the bottom line is that, like everything else in life, it's easier if you're happy."

Although I'm pretty certain my parishioner had never heard of the National Association of Social Workers' study on midlife women, her observation bears out their findings:

Menopause is not a major trauma for many midlife women. In fact, given some exceptions, most women report neutral or positive attitudes about menopause. This is not to minimize the physical changes that accompany menopause; however, research shows that the psychological impact of these signs is culture-bound. Educational interventions, for example, can lessen

*women's negative feelings about menopause and help
them cope better with the transition.*[1]

Regardless of how easy or hard we rate menopause, it's an undeniable physical transition. Physician Christiane Northrup writes about the brain and body changes that often accompany menopause: "There is much, much more to this midlife transformation than 'raging hormones.' Research into the physiological changes taking place in the perimenopausal woman is revealing that, in addition to the hormonal shift that means an end to childbearing, our bodies—and specifically, our nervous systems—are being, quite literally, rewired."[2]

For some women, this rewiring goes smoothly. For others, the side effects of the rewiring are cataclysmic. Almost all women claim that menopause brings a new clarity, with varying degrees of satisfaction and energizing anger. "I put all my significant relationships under a microscope," Northrup writes, and "began to heal the unfinished business from my past, experienced the first pangs of the empty nest, and established an entirely new and exciting relationship with my creativity and vocation."[3] But for Northrup—and for all of us—that transformation takes time and effort, and careful attention to our bodies and what they tell us.

MEDIEVAL HEALTH: AN OXYMORON?

Although beliefs about women's health have certainly changed since the Middle Ages, one constant is that women have always worked to be healthy. Medieval Europeans certainly had the odds stacked against them. Contaminated water and generally unsanitary conditions took many lives, regardless of station. Eleanor of Aquitaine's father, William, likely died from drinking polluted water while on pilgrimage to Compostela, Spain. (Eleanor herself—who would live into her early eighties—

introduced to Paris the civilizing practice of washing hands before serving meals.) Although diseases spread like wildfire before the contagious nature of disease was understood (most Europeans thought the Venicians were nuts for quarantining plague victims in 1348), infection was certainly not the only killer stalking the medieval Europeans. A dry summer or a harsh winter could spell famine for humans and livestock alike. People were more likely to die from accidents from which we easily recover today. Wars were frequent, and battlefield medicine was practically nonexistent. With the exception of outbreaks of the Black Death, the most common killer in medieval Europe was childbirth. Not much energy was spent on improving mortality rates for mothers and their babies, as the deaths were chalked up to Eve's misbehavior in the garden of Eden.

Even before 1347, when the most virulent of the plague epidemics is estimated to have decimated between a quarter and a third of the population, the population of western Europe was perhaps holding its own, but more likely declining due to the effects of disease, childbirth, war, and famine. On average, the European lifespan, taking into account those who died as babies or children, was around thirty during plague times and around forty without plagues. In the medieval world, it was a very old woman indeed who reached menopause—probably in her early forties.

Medieval medicine was based on the theory of humors, which has been around since Hippocrates (c. 460 BC–c. 377 BC). Just as there are four seasons governing nature, the theory went, so four humors or fluids govern health. The goal was balance among heat, cold, dryness, and moisture within the body. Patients who were sweaty and feverish were given cold, dry foods. Bloodletting, a common practice, was an attempt to bring the body back into balance. (This was so frequently prescribed that doctors outsourced the work to barbers, which is why they eventually adopted red and white striped poles, the red representing blood and the white representing the tourniquet.)

Over time, the concept of humors was applied to personality, and in the Middle Ages, melancholy was associated with a body that was too frequently cold and dry. (Maybe that's why a hot toddy perks you up!)

Lest you think medieval theories of medicine are extinct, recall American comedian Bill Cosby's routine in which he and his father are changing his newborn daughter's diaper. Grandpa chides Bill, "Isn't it *missing* something?" Just when you think we've progressed from the Middle Ages, someone has to go and view women as defective men again. I suppose this insistence that men are the norm and women the "other" reflects some fear of women—maybe especially fear of our power to bring forth life. When our childbearing days are over, it seems to make us even more frightening.

In 1584, an English justice of the peace named Reginald Scot published a book that was influential until the seventeenth century called *The Discoverie of Witchcraft*. In a place and time when menopausal women were especially at risk of being accused of witchcraft, having fulfilled their duty by bearing children, Scot may well have saved many lives. He threw witch hunters off balance with rational explanations of unusual occurrences and events with strategies like unveiling the secrets of magic tricks and blaming menopause. Scot believed it was common for women past their early to mid-forties, the medieval average for menopause in his day, to act oddly. Scot wasn't the last person to accuse menopausal women of strange behavior. But today, women at midlife are more likely to explain that we view the world with a new clarity.

Much of what medieval women knew about health came from other women—midwives and healers were the backbone of the health care system in the Middle Ages. Women were doctoring and nursing at birth beds and deathbeds until the rise of the university system around 1100, which gradually institutionalized medical training. Because women were excluded from medical training, their voices were slowly silenced, and the medical establishment increasingly viewed women's bodies as baby-making machines.

DR. HILDEGARD, MEDICINE WOMAN

Hildegard of Bingen—located in what is now southwestern Germany—expressed her vast creativity in varied ways, including the practice of medicine.

Living in a Benedictine monastery from early childhood, Hildegard was intimately familiar with the Rule of St. Benedict, which places great emphasis on healing the sick. In his sixth-century Rule, Benedict wrote, "Care of the sick must rank above and before all else, so that they may truly be served as Christ, for he said 'I was sick and you visited me'" (Matthew 25:36). The Rule required every monastery, whether inhabited by monks or nuns, to have infirmaries and a medical herb garden for the purpose of healing the sick and wounded.

Hildegard, the consummate multitasker, distinguished herself as an abbess renowned for her competence, a visionary theologian, a prophetic preacher, a pioneering musician, and a medical expert. Her existing work includes three books of visionary theology, eighty musical compositions, and a five-volume medical encyclopedia. She accepted the idea of the four humors, so her goal was keeping the four secretions of the body—yellow bile, blood, phlegm, and black bile—in balance, with treatments such as bloodletting, vomiting, sneezing, sweating, crying, and laxatives. Hildegard invented or otherwise approved of what we would call "all natural" remedies like compresses containing vinegar, mallow, oil, and sage for migraines—with which she herself was afflicted. One of Hildegard's medical volumes, which catalogs what was then known about herbs, plants, and their healing powers, is considered the earliest book on natural history written in German.

Hildegard's scholarly accomplishments continue to provide an invaluable history of medieval medicine. Her work also provides the basis of a thriving homeopathic practice in Germany, and some American researchers are exploring whether Hildegard's treatment for "madness" could shed light on cures for Alzheimer's and Parkinson's diseases. On a personal note, Hildegard's observation that sadness can lead to the cessation of menstruation rang true across the centuries for me, as it was three my years after my husband's death before my periods resumed.

But Hildegard's insistence that the body and the soul are indivisible is among her greatest contributions. And like a modern medical practitioner, she seemed eager to keep accusations of malpractice at bay: "The medicament given below were prescribed by God to be used against the above named ailments. Either they will heal the person or he will die if God does not will that he be healed."[4] But I'm not as cynical about her disclaimer as I once might have been. Although medieval people often blamed themselves and each other for disasters over which they had no control, and therefore imagined God as harshly judgmental, cruelly punitive, and eternally unforgiving, they always recognized God's constant presence—something we moderns often forget.

Hundreds of years before the term "holistic health" entered our vocabulary, Hildegard of Bingen knew exactly what that meant. She understood "that full health can only be experienced in a state of spiritual balance," as a medical doctor observed in 2002. "Psychological trauma, emotional distress, and other maladies of the soul often lead to illness and chronic diseases.

Healing the body begins with the self-healing of the spirit."[5] Hildegard herself claimed that the "Living Light" pitied her state of ill body and unwell soul while she resisted writing her visions.

Eventually, Hildegard was able to stop taking the blame for everything that went wrong. I suspect this important shift may have come about as she accepted her uniqueness as God's gift instead of as a burden. I also suspect this shift unlocked rivers of creativity and peace for her. Hildegard likely termed her health and resultant creativity as an alignment of the humors; the word "alignment" is key. Like Hildegard, most of us seem to learn the hard way that ignoring the interplay of mind, body, and soul compromises our mental, physical, and spiritual health.

HOLISTIC HEALTH FOR MEDIEVAL WOMEN

In the Middle Ages, people had a far deeper understanding of holistic health than we do today—they understood that relationship with God is integral to health. Can you imagine how a person from the Middle Ages would scoff at our outlandish claim that we completely control our lifespans through our diet, exercise, and other habits? Certainly, we have some control over our health and over how long we live, but the medievals knew the importance of being in *partnership* with God, not being God's replacement. Part of being a good partner with God is to adopt healthy habits like not smoking and examining our breasts monthly, which are simply ways of loving ourselves as created beings. Our medieval ancestors had no doubt that they were created by God, and that God was therefore intimately involved in their living and dying. Reminding ourselves of this medieval mindset can help us find balance in terms of taking care of ourselves. We're worth caring for because we're God's creations and, as such, we are never without God. Hildegard considered herself as a feather on the breath of God, and while we may chafe at the idea of being so passive, it's good to remember that the breath loves us and gives us life.

Jesus himself spoke to at least two mystics on the crucial interplay between body and soul, instructing Catherine of Siena that "visions that come from God inspire fear at first . . . but then go on to fortify. Visions of demonic origin yield sweetness at the outset, but soon pain and nausea develop. The certain sign that a vision is from God is that it will always bear fruit in 'a greater knowledge of truth in the soul.'"[6] In other words, the body plays a role in spiritual discernment. Listening to one's gut isn't a bad idea. Perhaps this is why Jesus advised Birgitta not to abuse her body for the sake of holiness. Instead, she was "to sleep sufficiently for bodily health; to be awake long enough for bodily exercise; to eat sufficiently for strength and physical well-being."[7]

THE MENOPAUSE BLUES

Like many menopausal women, Margery Kempe coped with copious tears. At first, Margery wept for herself. Later, she wept for others' suffering. She describes herself as having "wept wonder sore,"[8] for which she "suffered many a scorn, slander, banning and cursing."[9] As Margery tells it, in her Norfolk home-town then called Bishop's Lynn, now called King's Lynn,

> *many said there was never a saint in heaven who cried so as she did, wherefore they would conclude that she had a devil within her that caused that crying. . . . And then folk spitted at her for horror of the sickness, and some said that she howled like a dog and banned her and cursed her and said that she did much harm among the people. And then those who beforetime had given her both food and drink for God's love now put her away and bade her that she should not come in their places because of the sharp*

tales that they heard of her.[10]

Belgian mystic Marie d'Oignies (c. 1177–1213) had a similar experience with tears around two centuries before Margery's trials. After shedding many tears over being forced to marry at age fourteen (though she was later able to convince her husband to give up sexual relations and the couple dedicated their lives to caring for lepers), Marie wept uncontrollably during her visions, prayers, and meditations on the crucifix. A priest who fussed at Marie for her tears was himself stricken with weeping in the middle of preaching a sermon.

Margery's and Marie's experiences, as well as our own experiences with crying, highlight the truth that tears can offer a healing experience—which is probably how the term "a good cry" came into being. One thing's for sure, criticizing yourself or others for crying is neither helpful nor fair.

When considering applying for a position as a resident assistant (or, as the British say, a sub-warden) back in college, I was told that one of the worst things you can do when someone is weeping is to foist a box of tissues on him or her, because this communicates that the weeper should stop. It's much harder to sit with someone who's crying than to try to get the person to stop, but patience and a gentle, listening ear can be real gifts to a sad person.

Being with someone when she's having a crying jag can be a bonding experience. Even Margery, whose tears were so often a turnoff, learned the truth of this. On pilgrimage in Rome, though she "wept with great sobbing and loud crying" while meditating on the birth and childhood of Christ, Margery received comfort from other women, who tolerated her tears with understanding and kindness. "When these good women saw this creature [Margery] weep, sob, and cry so wonderfully and mightily that she was nearly overcome therewith, then they ordained a good soft bed and laid her thereupon and comforted her as much as they might. . . ."[11]

As time went by, Margery found that God was in her tears. She writes of herself, "And the more she busied herself to keep herself from crying, the louder she cried, for it was not in her power to take it or leave it, but as God would send it."[12] It seems to me that Margery's tears were anything but selfish, that they were somehow prayerful, a sort of physical manifestation of her care—and God's, too—for the sins and sufferings of the world.

The Bible is full of tears, with Jesus weeping over what he foresees as the destruction of Jerusalem (Luke 19:41) and at Lazarus's grave, even though he will restore his friend to life (John 11:35). And the lament psalms have images like God collecting tears in a divine bottle (Psalm 56:8) and the psalmist claiming, "My tears have been my food day and night" (Psalm 42:3). Psalms of lament give way to thanksgiving. It just isn't possible to skip the hard emotions to get to joy. And this is a piece of the wisdom our middle-aged tears offer. So take a page from Margery, who came to see her tears as gifts from God, and embrace your tears. They're part of being human (especially a menopausal woman-type human), and they're teachers, besides. Embrace your whole menopausal experience. It's part of who you are, and God longs for every part of you.

HEALTHY WISDOM, THEN AND NOW

Speaking from the thirteenth century, the poet-nun Mechthild of Magdeburg reminds us that our bodies are important, even on an eternal scale.

> Do not disdain your body, for the soul is just as safe in
> its body as in the kingdom of heaven—though not so certain.
> It is just as daring—but not so strong
> Just as powerful—but not so constant

Just as loving—but not so joyful
Just as gentle—but not so rich
Just as holy—but not yet so sinless
Just as content—but not so complete[13]

In some ways, Mechthild's advice sticks out against the backdrop of her fellow medieval mystics. Although Angela of Foligno was warned in an ecstasy that "not to eat or to eat very little" was a temptation,[14] many of her peers indulged in disturbing behavior.[15]

Nevertheless, there is much to learn from our mystics about the importance of treating our bodies kindly. Each section of Hildegard's *The Book of the Rewards of Life* begins with dialogues between a vice and its corresponding virtue. Here's the conversation Hildegard imagined between gluttony, the vice with which I'm most familiar, and restraint:

> *This image said: "God created all things. How then can I be spoiled by all these things? If God did not think these things were necessary, he would not have made them. Therefore, I would be a fool if I did not want these things, especially since God does not want man's flesh to fail."*
> [This is not unlike the very words I hear ice cream speaking to me nearly every night.]
> *Again I heard a voice responding to these words from the cloud. . . . It said: "No one should play a lyre in such a way that its strings are damaged. If its strings have been damaged, what sound will it make? None. You, gluttony, fill your belly so much that all your veins are bloated and are turned into a frenzy. Where then is the sweet sound of wisdom that God gave man?"*[16]

It's a wonderful message these mystics give us. Even those of us who eat too much ice cream and who think of a day without chocolate as a day without air can ask God for help. God wants us to enjoy food and God wants us to be healthy. So don't be afraid to ask God to feed you everything you need to live a life that is healthy in body, mind, and soul. As Christians, we need to remember that God is most perfectly revealed in the *body* of Jesus, a body that knew hunger, thirst, tears, suffering, and death. And so we can ask God without shame to be known in our imperfect bodies and our imperfect lives.

A PRAYER TO GET STARTED

God who created all the bodies of all creation, the bodies of the solar system, and even mine, thank you for the mystery of my body. Thank you for the beauty of my body even when my criticism blinds me to it. Thank you for the shapes and colors of my body that make it your unique creation. Help me to remember that you cherish my body, and so should I. Forgive me for disdaining my body. Forgive me for mistreating your gift of my body. Help me bring justice, wisdom, and peace to anyone who may have abused my body. Help all of us find the health you desire for us. In the name of you, whom Mechthild reminds us longed for us before the world began, Amen.

QUESTIONS FOR REFLECTION AND JOURNALING

1. Hildegard tells us that like billowing clouds and the incessant gurgle of the brook, the longing of the spirit can never be stilled. What does your body long for? What longings for health do you hear gurgling from your relationships, from your spirit?

2. Menopause is a time when a woman is forced to pay attention to her health. Recall other times in your life when you were forced to pay attention to your body. What happened during times when you've tried to ignore your body?

3. What do you know about your mother's menopause?

What have other women told or modeled about menopause for you? If you have a daughter, what would you tell her?

4. Here is Hildegard's visioning of herself as a feather on the breath of God. How does it speak to you in terms of how you desire to live your life?

> *Listen: there was once a king sitting on his throne. Around him stood great and wonderfully beautiful columns ornamented with ivory, bearing the banners of the king with great honor. Then it pleased the king to raise a small feather from the ground, and he commanded it to fly. The feather flew, not because of anything in itself but because the air bore it along. Thus am I, a feather on the breath of God.*[17]

5. We're so often urged to take control of our lives, and yet so frequently are inadequate to the task. How does the idea of allowing yourself to be born along on God's breath feel to you? Is there still room for you to be yourself?

4

GAL PALS

If you should find yourself in Bloomington, Indiana, make your way to Bloomington High School North (located on the north edge of town; the other high school is prosaically called "South") and look for a brick in the sidewalk—the kind that marks your donation to a good cause and offers the chance to proclaim your special message on it. The brick that is special to me reads:

JULIE RICH &

LISA BELCHER

BEST FRIENDS 4EVER

Of course, a brick could never contain all the shared secrets, the high drama of high school theater, the giggles, the tears, and the rolled eyes. But to me, this little piece of hardened clay symbolizes the way my friendship with Julie endured even when we had lost touch. Neither of us recalls a big blowup, though we certainly rode out our share of adolescent spats. We scheduled as many classes together as possible, called each other the minute we got off our respective school buses to catch up, and still had plenty to talk about at evening play rehearsals. Yet at some point, while attending different colleges less than an hour apart, we lost track of each other.

Fast-forward twenty years. I'm living in Fairfield, Connecticut, with my little boy, walking to the train station each morning for the daily commute to New York and excited at the prospect of getting a new car. The first hurdle was selling my old one, which was certainly old, but sturdy enough for someone who lived further from a train station than I to buy as a "station car." One caller from nearby Westport answered the ad I placed in the local paper and, on the test drive, I learned that his wife was Julie Rich. Ten minutes later, she and I were on the phone and, even today, she's still a person I can call anytime, to talk about anything, in any mood. Cancer has robbed both of us, Julie of her father and three older sisters, me of my first husband, and we like to think it was those who've gone before us who reunited us.

MEDIEVAL FRIENDSHIPS

The knowledge that friends are necessary in this life didn't escape women in the Middle Ages. When I first learned about Catherine of Siena's *bella brigata*, or "delightful gang," it took me right back to high school, and to the community or high school theater. My friends' and my passionate, dramatic temperaments were focused on producing high school standards like *Our Town*, *The Diary of Anne Frank*, *Oklahoma!* and *The Odd Couple*. Along the way, we became more tolerant of one another, more supportive of one another, more confident and competent, and less self-absorbed. I've often thought that church communities would do well to ask members where they've best experienced community. I'm sure that high school theater would be on many lists, and I know from experience that the community it provides has a lot to teach churches.

Catherine of Siena was one of those people who had a gift for being liked, in no small part because she had the gift for helping others discern God's voice in their spiritual lives. An informal group of followers who called themselves the *bella brigata* sprung up around her. A motley band from all accounts, they were men, women, young, old, rich, poor, ignorant, educated, ordained, lay, professionals, unemployed, who gradually became a force to be reckoned with in medieval Siena and beyond. They became the go-to group if you were struck by the plague, out of money, out of food, or otherwise down on your luck, and twenty-three of them accompanied Catherine on her official mission to Avignon when she sought to heal the church's schism over two popes.

Nevertheless, nasty rumors swirled around Siena, fueled by the fact that both men and women, some married, some not, followed Catherine. Offended neighbors nicknamed them the "Caterinati," roughly translated as "bewitched by Catherine." Yet the friends took up the name, as well as Catherine's ideals and courage—she insisted that Christ's love for us is so strong that love, not nails, held him to the cross—that they began to wear the moniker with pride. And on August 15, 1992, Rome official-ly recognized the International Association of Caterinati as an international association of the faithful.

A century or so before the *bella brigata*, Clare of Assisi (1194–1253) modeled the importance of one-on-one friendship in her platonic relationship with the better-known Francis (1181–1226). Their story—both of them born into leading Assisi families who didn't understand their disdain of wealth, and both of them strikingly good-looking—is irresistible. Beneath the glamour of their story, however, are two people who struggled to live in the light of a revealed God. Clare's obstinate insistence on poverty is legendary. Both Clare and Francis burned with conviction that the church of their day found a bit excessive. Without one another to call on occasionally (some-times years passed between visits) for advice, would Clare have been able to stand up to the pope? After Francis's death, Pope Gregory IX sought to sever relations between the orders Francis and Clare had founded. No doubt, Clare's conviction that the relationship between the all-male and all-female orders was healthy and important came from the abiding friendship she and Francis had known. For instance, Francis had successfully persuaded Clare to keep her fasting and bodily penance in check. And Francis had relied on Clare's intuition when it came to judging applicants to his order. She's also credited with encouraging Frances to answer the call to become a mendicant, a traveling preacher who has taken a vow of poverty and must depend on begging to survive.

SISTERHOOD

Given the importance of connection, the scarcity of choice for women in the Middle Ages, the dangers of dying in childbirth, and the enormous influence of the church, no wonder the religious life appealed to some. Yet becoming a nun was no guarantee of an easy life. Any young woman who thought she was escaping the sleepless nights faced by new mothers was in for a shock, as a medieval nun's day began at two in the morning with Matins, although she was allowed to go back to bed and sleep until six, when Prime began. Silence was kept nearly every hour of the day, even at meals. Communicating silently was a creative endeavor. Historian Eileen Power writes, "A sister who wanted fish would wag her hands displayed sidelings in the manner of a fish tail; if she wanted to say 'pass the milk,' she would draw her little finger in the manner of milking." Likewise, "a guilty sacristan struck by the thought that she had not provided incense for mass would put her fingers into her nostrils."[1]

Although there were certainly women who chose to be nuns, Clare among them, most had the choice thrust upon them.

Hildegard's parents considered her, their tenth child, a human tithe to the church, and so she entered a convent at the age of eight. Like most medieval nuns, Hildegard came from a wealthy family. Working girls, of course, helped run country farms and urban businesses, and their families couldn't afford the dowry. But there must have been plenty of opportunities for friendship with coworkers. Women of the nobility, who tended to be more isolated, were probably the least likely to develop friendships, so surely some of the genteel ladies who found themselves in convents thanked God for female companionship they might have been more hard-pressed to find had they been married to a noble instead of to Christ.

THE BEGUINES: OUTSIDE THE BOX

Some ingenious medieval women brought together the best of the community of religious life into the wider world—without the entrance fees. They were the Beguines. If Catherine of Siena's *bella brigata* was criticized for fraternizing with friends of the opposite sex, no matter how nonsexual their relationships, you can imagine what the Beguines, groups of women who lived together without the blessing of the church, were in for. It must have taken healthy self-esteem—or cheering from supportive friends—to choose this relatively independent way of life.

Beguine Mechthild of Magdeburg, Germany, seems to have been a confident woman. She also seems have understood the blessings, as well as the complications, that the vulnerability of friendship brings. Born around 1210, Mechthild apparently had an easier time hearing her own voice than many of us, and it seems she never lost the sound of God's. At puberty, Mechthild declared she was greeted by the Holy Spirit, and thereafter saw "all things in God and God in all things." The Holy Spirit soon became like a neighbor who didn't need to knock, and

Mechthild claimed that the Holy Spirit dropped by every day. Among Mechthild's writing is this lovely description of the Holy Spirit that reminds me of haiku:

> *The Holy Spirit is our harpist*
> *and all the strings*
> *which*
> *are touched in love Must sound.*[2]

Mechthild had a powerful urge to be herself (notice her use of the word "must"). Because Mechthild was interested in taking the veil of neither wife nor nun, at twenty-something she left home for Magdeburg, in what is now north-central Germany, where she knew no one. To those who questioned her decision, she explained, "The true greeting of God, which comes from the heavenly flood out of the spring of the flowing Trinity, has such power that it takes all strength from the body and lays the soul bare to itself."[3]

Mechthild's life was marked by criticism for her independent actions and notions, and she didn't seem to bear the criticism easily. Perhaps she had led a sheltered childhood that left her ill prepared for the criticism her choices would incur; in any event, she drew strength from the memory of family and friends "to whom I was most dear."[4] Choosing to become a Beguine was a suspect, though not unheard of, decision. Between the twelfth and fourteenth centuries, maidens and widows throughout Europe banded together to live lives of prayer and service, vowing poverty and lifelong celibacy if unmarried. The etymology of the term "Beguine" is uncertain. It may come from the old Flemish word for "to pray." In addition to praying, soberly clad Beguines worked among the sick and the poor, establishing hospitals, caring for the elderly, ministering to the dying, and teaching the young. Some lived with their families. Some lived together in households of fifteen or so. Many formed large, self-sufficient settlements within cities. Even the Beguines' critics seem to have found them uniformly, undeniably pious, yet "Beguine" was sometimes used as derogatory term.

The Beguines didn't seem to know a woman's place. They ignored the convention that women were to live under the guardianship of fathers, husbands, brothers, priests, and popes. Usually, Beguine settlements were established with support from wealthy women and, with time, they became economically independent, their members supporting themselves as teachers, manual laborers, and even in the decidedly unfeminine world of the cloth trade.

Beguinages—the villages within cities where many Beguines lived—were sometimes quite elaborate, and housed up to fourteen thousand members. Often walled, beguinages were usually built around a courtyard surrounded by buildings that included a church (sometimes more than one), a hospital, a nursing home, a cemetery, a school, and, in at least one case, a brewery. Modest homes where Beguines lived lay behind the buildings for work and worship.

These unconventional women didn't acknowledge a founder, didn't have a constitution, didn't live under a religious Rule, and it's debatable whether they wore religious clothing. A thirteenth-century friar wrote, "There are among us women whom we have no idea what to call, ordinary women or nuns, because they live neither in the world nor out of it."[5] Some Beguines were authors, often writing in the vernacular rather than in Latin. Mechthild herself was the first woman to write in medieval German. In short, Beguines threatened church bureaucracy by their out-of-the-box approach to Christianity.

In 1273, a bishop wrote the pope (in Latin, of course) that if *he* had papal authority, he would have the Beguines "married or thrust into an approved order." In 1312, an ecclesial council declared, "Their way of life is to be permanently forbidden and altogether excluded from the Church of God."[6] By then, when it was dangerous to be a Beguine, Mechthild had been dead for around a quarter of a century; in her day, Beguines were generally just considered eccentric and brave enough to curry no favor with the established church.

Being a Beguine offered unmarried women community without the confinement of a convent and relationships with those to whom they ministered. Sometimes, friendship arrived in the form of a spiritual advisor. Mechthild's relationship with Heinrich von Halle, a Dominican brother, was as lasting as Clare's was with Francis, even after Mechthild resisted Heinrich's encouragement to write down her mystical experiences. Heinrich translated Mechthild's work into Latin, giving it a larger readership. A Latin copy fell into the hands of Dante, who was influenced by Mechthild's concept of divine light. Some even claim that Dante based Matilda, the personification of mysticism in *The Purgatorio*, on Mechthild of Magdeburg.[7]

Despite Dante's admiration, Mechthild's writing was severely criticized. In the first place, few men were as forward thinking as Heinrich, particularly when it came to the Beguines. Like her sister Beguines, Mechthild experienced God on a very personal, even intimate level, which led the authorities to fuss over "the heresy of the free spirit," the belief that a relationship with God is possible without meddling from clergy or guardians (fathers, husbands, brothers).

It may have been as punishment for the heresy of possessing a free spirit that Mechthild was first denied communion at age thirty. Her sharp tongue may have played a role as well. The author of gentle, assuring images of God did not think highly of clerics, and she counted no friends inside the church they ran. Mechthild claimed that "God calls the cathedral clergy 'goats' because their flesh stinks of impurity with regard to eternal truth." As for the church of the "goats," Mechthild said it was "filthy, for she is unclean and unchaste."

Although Mechthild continued to write, it was with agitation rather than with an easy confidence.

> *I was warned against writing this book. People said if I did not watch out, it could be burned. So I did as I used to do as a child. When I was sad, I always had to pray. I bowed to my Lover and said: "Alas, Lord, now I am saddened all because of your honor. If I am going to receive no comfort from you now, then you led me astray, because you are the one who told me to write it." At once God revealed himself to my joyless soul, held this book in his right hand, and said, "My dear one, do not be overly troubled. No one can burn the truth. . . . The words symbolize my marvelous Godhead. It flows continuously into your soul from my divine mouth. The sound of the words is a sign of my living spirit and through it achieves genuine truth. Now examine all these words— how admirably do they proclaim my personal secrets! So have no doubts about yourself."*

Mechthild's response, while understandable, is somewhat on the whiny side. "Ah, Lord, if I were a learned religious man, and if you had performed this unique miracle using him, You would receive everlasting honor for it." God's response is something you're unlikely to hear in a classroom, but I for one am glad Mechthild recorded it. "One finds many a professor learned in scripture who actually is a fool in My eyes. And I'll tell you something else: It is a great honor for Me with regard to them, and it very much strengthens Holy Christianity that the unlearned tongue, aided by My Holy Spirit, teaches the learned tongue."[8] More words that inflamed the authorities and their learned tongues, and Mechthild's conflict with them may have contributed to her decline in health. Though Mechthild's inner hearing remained clear throughout her life, her vision failed her.

Mechthild left the Beguine community in Magdeburg in her sixties after a series of unfortunate incidents. Obviously so deeply hurt she felt the unknown was a better choice than the status quo, Mechthild reveals this much:

> *All the days of my life before I began this book and before a single word of it had come into my soul, I was one of the most naive people ever to be in religious life. I knew nothing about the devil's malice; I was unaware of the frailty of the world; the duplicity of people in religious life was also unknown to me.*[9]

Even in Mechthild's thirteenth century, friendships sometimes soured.

Feeling herself a "post or target at which people throw stones" and by now forbidden all holy rites as punishment for going public with her spiritual experiences, Mechthild was relieved to be taken in at the well-known convent in Helfta, though it meant undertaking the longest journey of her life: fifty miles. She was well cared for by the nuns there, teaching us that we can find and make new friends at any age. Shortly after her arrival, she went blind; she dictated the last in the series of seven books of *The Flowing Light of the Godhead*. Some scholars believe faithful Heinrich came to take Mechthild's dictation.

Mechthild is an example of a woman whose own unique voice seems to be deeply rooted in God's. But it would be interesting to ask Mechthild, face to face, if she ever grappled to hear her own voice. How frequently, and what was it like? I wonder how steady she seemed to her friends. Why were these friendships unable to be maintained? Clearly, Mechthild knew conflict—through clashes with those who wanted to burn her books, with those who denied her communion, with those hurt her so badly she was compelled, though in ill health and elderly by the standards of her day, to leave the beguinage in Magdeburg where she had spent the bulk of her life. If we could speak with Mechthild, I bet she'd remind us that one's own voice surfaces in the midst of conflict, and that one's voice is best heard in the context of good friends.

MIDLIFE FRIENDSHIP, THEN AND NOW

The Beguines are often nicknamed "the order that was no order." In their dedication to assuming a structure only if it made sense for them, they remind me of today's Red Hatters. Finished with parent-teacher association politics and fed up with committee work, members of the Red Hat Society, all women over the age of fifty, proclaim a joyful dedication to dis-organization—and to the importance of female friends. Sue Ellen Cooper, founder and "Queen Mother" of the phenomenon, writes,

> *We need to find new, more palatable ways to age. Since we have no role models to show us how to do this, we are peer mentoring, looking at one another and saying, "Now how do we do this?" We are watching and consulting one another, figuring out how to age without acting old. Surely, we can reinvent the process of aging to suit ourselves, or at least find a way to make it more user-friendly.*[10]

The Red Hat Society takes its name from the wonderful poem, "Warning—When I Am an Old Woman I Shall Wear Purple" by the British poet Jenny Joseph that continues, "with a red hat that doesn't go."

A recent BBC poll named "Warning" the most popular twentieth-century poem in the United Kingdom, and the Red Hat Society has transformed the poem into a call to arms. Attired in purple clothing and red hats (lilac and pink if you're under fifty), Red Hatters pride themselves on having a good time in "dis-organized" chapters with playful names like Better Red than Dead and the Varicose Vixens. Their purpose is to enjoy each other and life with other women whose friendship networks of children's schools, workplace, and neighborhoods may have shifted. Of the over one million women in roughly two dozen countries who call themselves Red Hatters, American Anne Abernathy may be the most famous—she wore a purple-striped red helmet as she competed in the 2006 Winter Olympics.

Another growing phenomenon is the girlfriend weekend, where women who may or may not know each other take over an inn for the weekend. Activities range from scrapbooking to snowboarding to discussing Jane Austen to shopping to spa visits.

Sacramento Bee reporter Cynthia Hubert interviewed a variety of psychologists and other experts on women's friendships, and she concludes that "in general ... men's friendships are based on common interests or skills, while women's are based on sharing feelings," which could explain why my fiancé likes to get together with a couple of buddies to fish, while I treasure friends with whom I talk and e-mail about our emotional lives. Hubert also reports that "depth of emotion and lack of fear are the essence of what makes women's friendships different than men's"—which is borne out by the experience of Margery of Kempe. Brushed aside by a male confessor who refused to hear her out, she turned to Julian of Norwich, who was perhaps less fearful of Margery's deep and dramatic emotions.

Finally, Hubert notes the health benefits of friendship, citing a study that found that socially isolated rats' chances of developing breast cancer increase by 40 percent.[11] This could explain my casual observation from my friendships with the sisters of St. Margaret, an Episcopal women's order, that women who are dedicated to communal life seem to live a long, long time.

A wise therapist once told me she defines as therapy as the process of hearing oneself clearly. This is the gift Julie and my other friends are for me. Of course, they cost a whole lot less than therapy, and are a good deal more fun. They allow me to hear myself better than I can without them—and the clearing created in my soul gives me more room for God.

A PRAYER TO GET STARTED

God of every friend we've ever had or lost or wanted or needed or loved, thank you for every one of them. Thank you for the Beguines and their model of female friendship. Thank you especially for Beguine Mechthild of Magdeburg and her courage to pursue her friendship with you. Thank you for her reminder that we live in you as a spark lives in a flame. Thank you for her ability to express herself and for her willingness to share her understanding of you with us. Help us find our own true voice to lead us into the relationship with you we are created to enjoy, and give us the willingness to share our experience of you with our friends. In the name of you, whom Mechthild told us is "as morning dew to summer flowers," Amen.

QUESTIONS FOR JOURNALING AND REFLECTION

1. Beguines like Mechthild of Magdeburg were simultaneously admired and loathed. Why do you think they were eventually extinguished, instead of encouraged? How do you feel about the Beguines' example?
2. Many Beguines lived in beguinages, communities designed to facilitate the women's ministries. If you were

designing a beguinage, what would it look like? What kinds of services would it provide? What kind of environment would it offer? Who would live in your beguinage? (It's your beguinage, so men are welcome if you like.) Feel free to draw a map and a list of guidelines for those who live in your imaginary beguinage. How would friendships be nurtured there?

3. Mechthild embarked on two life-changing journeys, one to Magdeburg to become a Beguine in her early twenties, and the second to enter the convent at Helfta toward the end of her life. What do you think these journeys represented to her, and do you think her age had anything to do with it? What do you think Mechthild's older self would tell her younger self as she set out on the first journey? Have you made similar life-changing journeys? What were you fleeing? Were you leaving reluctantly? Joyfully? Were you in a hurry? Dragging your feet? What were you glad to be rid of? What was the most precious thing you found? Did your age play a role in how you experienced the journey?

4. Spend some time thinking about your friends. If you could bring them all together for a party, who would most enjoy each other? Who is the first friend you remember having? As you recall friends from school, from jobs, from places where you once lived, what do they have in common? How have your friends nourished your faith or helped you to grow? What does your choice of friends tell you about your life?

5

DEPRESSION AND OTHER NASTIES

For me, depression feels like I'm drowning in a can of paint. Depression is thick, its odor is suffocating, and its color is simultaneously bland and ugly. The only attractive thing that exists in the world is sleep. Nothing, nothing else even comes close to being interesting. Then there's depression's kissing cousin, anxiety. Anxiety is a real showstopper. It stops me from sleeping. Stops me from enjoying. Anxiety seeks to control everything— what to eat, what to wear, what to say, what to do—from behind its screen. Like the Wizard of Oz, anxiety quivers with worry and fear, but is powerful nevertheless. Both depression and anxiety consume: anxiety like a Pacman chasing my soul, depression luring me into a cave familiar in its loneliness. If I had to know so much about depression and anxiety, I wish it were from the outside instead of from the inside.

Episcopal priest Barbara Cawthorne Crafton writes in her online column that the "enemy" psalms, the often distasteful, uncomfortable-making psalms that "ask God to rain down all manner of horror upon unnamed foes," are helpful. She observes,

They're pretty graphic, these songs—especially when you reflect upon the fact that they were probably sung in worship services. . . . I know they're awful. But . . . the blood-and-guts psalms help: "Have mercy on me, O God, for my enemies are hounding me; all day long they assault and oppress me" [Psalm 56:1]. The jerks. I don't know why it happens, but the spirits of sadness and worthlessness just show up sometimes. The jerks.

I am not without help. This has happened before and "He will send forth heaven and save me; he will confound those who trample upon me" [Psalm 57:3]. . . . Hee hee. I can't wait. I feel better just thinking about it."[1]

I think Crafton is really onto something. As Ellen Davis, a divinity school professor of mine, advised, the psalms can be so helpful it's not bad advice to "Take two psalms and call me in the morning."[2] When anxiety, depression, or difficult people get me down, I can always borrow this prayer from the psalms: "How long shall the wicked triumph? They bluster in their insolence; all evildoers are full of boasting" (Psalm 94:4–5).

Let the psychiatrists haggle over the reasons—suppressed anger, bad genes, overload from caring for too many people (except yourself), molestation, too many conflicting expectations—the fact is, women are twice as likely as men to develop depression. And as many as one in three of us become clinically depressed at some point in our lives.[3]

If you're reading this book and struggling with severe depression, I want you to get help. Now. Killing yourself can wait. Pick up the phone and call 1-800-SUICIDE. Now. If you're deaf, call 1-800-799-4TTY. Now. There is help, and there is hope. And I'm praying for you. In the meantime, thumb through those psalms.

Depression, anxiety, and other mental anguish are not signs of spiritual weakness. That idea is as medieval as the view that the Black Death was caused by sin. Sometimes it seems that those who need to find meaning in our lives are more prone to depression and similar nasties. The spiritual quest for meaning sometimes *starts* with depression or with lacking belief in meaning. Take a look at Jesus' forty days of temptation in the wilderness. Shortly after Jesus' baptism, the Holy Spirit led Jesus to the desert, where Satan let him have it. Scholars who pick apart the Greek texts point out that the Holy Spirit doesn't merely encourage Jesus but *compels* him toward this harsh, desolate, lonely place. All ends happily enough. Jesus is strengthened, so he resists the devil and the angels minister to him (Matthew 4:1–11; Mark 1:12–13; Luke 4:1–13). But the successful conclusion is not to say that Jesus' fortifying ordeal was easy. Neither is depression. Remember that. And remember also that none of us is alone in our particular desert.

DEALING WITH DEPRESSION IN THE MIDDLE AGES

Teresa of Avila, though known for her excellent sense of humor (upon viewing the only portrait of herself painted in her lifetime, she is said to have told the friar-artist, "May God forgive you, for you have made me look ugly and bleary-eyed"), is also known to have experienced depression. Following a deep depression, Teresa began having visions of Christ at age forty and, though this was not an easy experience, she was strengthened enough to spend the last twenty years of her life establishing sixteen monasteries throughout Spain based on her intimate relationship with Jesus. At age fifty-eight, Teresa had a difficult experience founding a community for nuns in Salamanca.

Teresa later reflected on that challenge to the nuns she led. "We moved on the eve of St. Michael, a little before dawn," she writes:

The news had already been spread that . . . a sermon would be preached [and therefore the town leaders would come]. . . . [O]n the afternoon of that day we moved it rained so hard that it was most difficult to bring the things we needed. The chapel had been newly fixed up, but the roof was so poorly tiled that the rain came through most of it. I tell you, daughters, I felt very imperfect that day. Since the news had already been spread about [concerning the sermon], I didn't know what to do. I became so distressed that I said to the Lord, almost complaining, that either He not order me to get involved in repair works or He help me in this need.[4]

This little passage reveals several things about Teresa that make me like her and look up to her. First, she was honest about feeling "very imperfect," even though she was to set an example for her followers, to whom she confessed her very human feeling. Secondly, Teresa got anxious and overcome. And thirdly, when she did, she took her frustration and depression to the Lord.

Margery of Kempe wrote of herself during a time when she was at her wit's end, apparently suffering from a severe case of postpartum depression after the birth of her first child:

She would have killed herself many a time because of her stirrings . . . and as a witness thereof she bit her own hand so violently that it was seen all her life afterward. And also she tore the skin on her own body against her heart grievously with her nails, for she had no other instruments, and worse she would have done, save she was bound and kept with strength both day and night so that she might not have her will.[5]

Suicidal, self-mutilating—to describe Margery as deeply

depressed is an understatement. Yet, when "men thought she should never have escaped nor lived . . . as she lay alone and her keepers were away from her, our merciful Lord Christ Jesus, ever to be trusted . . . never forsaking his servant in time of need, appeared to his creature."[6] Margery's life was changed forever, though she writes honestly of her struggles with her emotions, her behavior, and her faith throughout her long life. In a way, Margery's groundbreaking *The Book of Margery Kempe* is a story of courage in which she uses her own trials to inspire others, much like former American First Lady Betty Ford or Britain's late Princess Diana. Margery's is also a story of going to God—or rather, of God coming to her—when she was out of places to run.

Teresa used her honesty about her difficulties and her willingness to take them to God to write "Nada te turbe," the poem that has comforted so many and that has inspired an especially lovely Taizé chant.

> *Let nothing upset you,*
> *let nothing startle you.*
> *All things pass;*
> *God does not change.*
> *Patience wins*
> *all it seeks.*
> *Whoever has God*
> *lacks nothing;*
> *God alone is enough.*[7]

Teresa and Margery demonstrate the hard truth that faith does not insulate us from depression and anxiety. But both these mystics also show us how helpful honest faith can be as we cope with these nasties. A 2002 study by the American Psychiatric Association bears this out, especially for depressed seniors. Those "who believe their life is guided by a larger spiritual force have significantly fewer symptoms of depression than those who do not use religious coping strategies. Moreover, this relationship is independent of the amount of social support those individuals receive." As medical doctor and Duke University professor Harold G. Koenig comments, "This is a pretty remarkable study—and when you see these kind of data coming out from both medical and psychiatric populations, it's hard to continue ignoring religion as a variable in the recovery from depression."[8] So don't give up wrestling with God.

As most people of faith, any faith, will tell you, God does not prevent suffering, but God is present through it all. Julian of Norwich attests, "These words, 'you will not be overcome,' were said very insistently and strongly [by Jesus], for certainty and strength against every tribulation which may come. He did not say, 'You will not be assailed, you will not be belabored, you will not be disquieted,' but he said, 'You will not be overcome.'"[9]

It's the way Julian pestered God, asking incessantly why bad things happen to good people, that first drew me to her within my first years as a young widow. Gradually, Julian became convinced of God's love and learned that suffering's gift is wisdom. She wrote,

> *In endless love we are led and protected by God, and we never shall be lost; for he wants us to know that soul is a life, which life of his goodness and his grace will last in heaven without end, loving him, thanking him, praising him. And just as we were to be without end, so we were treasured and hidden in God, known and loved from without beginning.*[10]

Over time, Julian was content in the conviction that "all things shall be well and all manner of things shall be well,"[11] but it was a hard-won conviction that never denied suffering. The trick, Julian shared with us, is constantly to remind ourselves that we are not alone. She recalled,

> *Once my understanding was let down into the bottom of the sea, and there I saw green hills and valleys, with the appearance of moss, strewn with seaweed and gravel. Then I understood in this way: that if a man or woman were there under the wide waters, if he could see God, as God is continually with man [and woman], he would be safe in soul and body, and come to no harm. And furthermore, he would have more consolation and strength than all this world can tell.*[12]

When you are drowning in depression, anxiety, or any kind of suffering, let your imagination do you a favor and close your eyes to imagine Jesus with you, holding your hand, stroking your forehead as if you were a fevered child. A friend of mine, Lorraine, once underwent surgery. The situation wasn't considered life threatening, but she was terrified nevertheless, even writing a letter the night before to her husband and young children. Lorraine felt relieved when it turned out the operating room nurse was a family friend. Afterward, she told the friend how much she appreciated her presence, "especially your holding my hand during the surgery." "Lorraine," the friend answered, "I'm glad I could be here, but I wasn't holding your hand." And immediately Lorraine knew: it was *Jesus* holding her hand. She still had to face the ordeal of surgery, but she didn't have to face it alone.

I had a slower-growing mystical experience the year I commuted each morning to a job that had become so uncertain I didn't know if I would be employed at the end of the day. Sadly, it was a job I had once loved, and thankfully, my colleagues and I were able to support one another during the very stressful reign of a new boss. So God was present to me through those colleagues. But God was also present to me in helping me grow in a surprising way during this very anxious time. To steel myself for whatever the day would bring (and energize myself for finding a new job), I silently prayed Morning Prayer on the subway. And to put the day behind me so I could put my energies into being a good mother, I prayed Evening Prayer on the way home.

All the Daily Offices use the psalms abundantly, and as anyone who has spent much time with the psalms can tell you, they give you permission to rail at God. There's no need to worry about self-pity when you're praying the psalms. So maybe it was because I had permission to whine, to be perfectly honest about the depths of my anger, anxiety, and fear, that a mystical thing happened. I found myself becoming, of all things, *grateful*. Grateful for my little boy, though furious that his father had died when he was only twenty-six months old. Grateful for a job, though furious that it had gone so sour. Grateful for my life, though furious that it was so exhaustingly hard at the moment. Since that awful time at work (yes, times like those *do* pass), I've learned that gratitude, though oddly bitter to swallow, is good medicine for depression.

ELISABETH: PRAYING HER WAY THROUGH DEPRESSION

Like Margery of fourteenth- and fifteenth-century England, Elisabeth of thirteenth-century Schonau, Germany, was weighed down by the gravity of darkness, in the depths of a paralyzing, suicidal depression, when she received visions that lifted her out of her depression and transformed her into a prophet. Elisabeth wrote of the depression that seemed to come from out of nowhere:

I remained all day in a certain darkness of soul. On the next day also, and for the whole week, I was sad and went along in the same darkness, unable to shake off that melancholy. . . . Amid all this, I was also afflicted with so great a weariness that there was nothing that my soul did not loathe. The prayers that used to be my greatest pleasure were annoying to me. The Psalter, which had always been a great joy to me, I threw far from me when I had hardly finished reading one psalm. . . . The Betrayer even made me hesitate in my faith so that I pondered our Redeemer with skepticism . . . my Adversary so much more strongly pressed on, disturbing me in such a way that it even wearied me to live. . . . Finally, that Betrayer inspired me to put an end to my life and thereby terminate the tribulations I had endured for so long. But at this worst temptation, the one who defends Israel did not sleep.[13]

The nuns and monks in Elisabeth's convent poured on the prayer and, finally, after nearly two years (between Pentecost 1152 and the day before Palm Sunday, 1154) of severe depression, while

I was lying prostrate in prayer with the sisters . . . my heart was enlarged and I saw a great light in the heavens . . . After a little while, the angel of the Lord came, and quickly raised me up and stood me on my feet, saying, "O person, rise, stand on your feet, and I will speak with you, and do not be afraid, because I am with you all the days of your life."

Elisabeth did indeed experience a friendship with the divine. For the rest of her life, she conversed with angels and others inhabiting eternity, including some relatives, the Virgin Mary, and St. Peter. Often, Elisabeth's visions occurred in "a place of most charming pleasantness," full of green meadows, mountains, and smelling sweetly. God told her that in her illness, "I have blessed you and filled you with light and opened your eyes that you might see, not through ordinary sight, but through knowledge of God."[14]

Elisabeth strikes me as a remarkably pious soul. Although most Christians in the Middle Ages tended to date things by the church calendar, referring to, for instance, the feast of Sts. Peter and Paul instead of to June 29, Elisabeth drew parallels with those who are being commemorated and her experiences. Her questions weren't as deep or as insistent as Julian's had been. She was more likely to ask the Virgin Mary, "How old were you when you learned you were going to give birth to Jesus?"[15] than "Why does suffering exist?" But, freed of depression, her curiosity returned, and Elisabeth exhibited the same freedom as Julian in asking whatever was on her mind.

DEALING WITH DEPRESSION, THEN AND NOW

Although no one in her right mind would ever want them, there *are* gifts of depression. Do you remember Spirographs? Using gears and pins and patience, you could draw original designs. One Christmas, my artistic mother determined that I should have the toy, although I had no interest in it. The Christmas before, my uncle and aunt had given me the first books in *The Wind and the Willows* series, and I was hoping they'd give me the next few installments this year. But the present from them that Christmas was suspiciously the size of a Spirograph box, and I thought I was being polite when, upon opening it, I exclaimed, "Oh boy! Just what Mom wanted me to get!" I wish I could tell you that this unwanted toy launched me on a brilliant career as an architect, but that would be a lie. But though I was obviously not a brilliant artist, I enjoyed the toy more than I thought I would.

Sometimes you get presents you don't want, but you might as well do what you can with them anyway. To repeat, depression, which no one in her right mind would ever want, comes with gifts nevertheless. One of the unwanted presents happens when depression rips the "nice girl" persona most of us wear too frequently from its hanger and leaves it crumpled in a forgotten heap in the back of the closet. Minus the nice girl costume, we lose our inhibitions against duking it out with God. And the gift is that, like Elisabeth, we find our spiritual lives forever enriched.

Struggling with depression and other nasties can give us a sense of how little power they have. The mystics assure us that evil is a reality. Teresa recounted that Satan stunk of brimstone, and that when she saw him perched on her prayer book, he skittered away when she tossed holy water on him. Julian saw the Fiend as "red with black freckles, which clutched at her throat with its paws."[16] As Julian was so completely dehabilitated by her experience of Christ's passion that she was thought to be on her deathbed, it must have seemed extraordinarily odd when she did the unthinkable. Julian laughed. She chortled, giggled, tee-heed and guffawed—though on the brink of death. Having undergone the passion with Christ, Julian wrote that Jesus, "without voice or speech . . . framed in [her] soul these words: 'By this is the Fiend overcome.'" Julian understood that Christ's passion trumps the Fiend's evil ways every time.

> [H]e can never do all the evil that he wants. His power is in God's control. . . . I saw our Lord scorn such malice, and expose the emptiness of the Fiend's powerlessness; and it is his will that we should do the same. When I saw this, I laughed so heartily that it made those around me

laugh too, and their laughter did me good. I thought
I would have liked all my fellow Christians to have seen
what I saw, that they might laugh with him.[17]

Julian claimed that it pleases Christ when we're able to laugh
at the devil, as this is rejoicing with God that the Fiend has been
conquered by Christ's sacrifice.

A friend told me of the release she found when she confid-
ed to her grown niece that she was very upset by a family member. "You're kidding! *She* of all people upsets you?" the younger
woman responded. "In the first place, she's horsey looking.
In the second place, she wears more mascara than Tammy Faye.
In the third place, she's *way* too old to be wearing Laura Ashley,
which just makes her look like she's in the middle of
a sex-change experience." Since recovering from her laughter, my
friend has felt less intimidated by this relative and is more
accepting of her. So when I told her about "our" mystics laughing at the devil, she said, "Well, they're right—a good laugh really does take the power out of whatever it is that's eating you."

Mystics such as Elisabeth, Teresa, Margery, and Julian reveal
that, somehow, the deeper your capacity for suffering, the deeper your capacity for joy. While you're in the midst of depression
or anxiety, though, it's hard to remember that joy is the other side
of the coin. Barbara Crafton advises, "Sometimes it helps us
grasp the possibility of God's love if we choose to proceed for a
time as if it were true, to take the love of God as a working
hypothesis in life and see what happens. And what happens is
this: more and more things begin to look like love. The good and
the beautiful begin to seem intentional."[18]

As I learn more about "our" mystics, I realize how different
they are from one another. Elisabeth would be the one to hold
me spellbound as she described her visions. Teresa is the one
I would want to share a laugh with. Julian I would choose for a

therapist. But all of them are good companions for any of us who make our way through depression and anxiety.

Because God seems to be revealed in ways that are as unique as each of our mystics, none of us needs to be all things to all people. I think the outrageous expectations many middle-aged women live under—to be the top sales rep, the mother whose children have no problems, the strongest pillar of church and community, both grandmother and lover of the year—are often root causes of depression. I've heard some wonderfully wise people claim that serenity is when you're happy to be one of the grains of the sand of life.

Just being ourselves is enough. We don't have to be everything. None of "our" mystics seem to have sought to be anyone other than themselves. Margery stayed herself even when it drove others berserk. Julian stayed put in her cell and meditated, Theresa traipsed all over Spain founding convents. Elisabeth's fellow nuns were the original beneficiaries of her visionary gifts, while Julian wanted to share hers with her fellow "even-Christians." They wouldn't tell you that learning to be yourself is easy, but they would tell you that you're not alone, and that being yourself is a great gift to God, to the world, and to yourself. They would also add that each of us is a gift, no matter what our mood happens to be.

A PRAYER TO GET STARTED

God, who is our Creator no matter what our mood, thank you for making us complex. Thank you for giving us our lives to learn about ourselves. Thank you for loving us even when we have a hard time loving ourselves or anyone else. Thank you especially for Elisabeth of Schonau and her openness about the bewildering pain of depression. Thank you, also, for the psalms and the permission they give us to fully experience the range of human emotion. Give us hope that our painful feelings, like Elisabeth's, will give way to growth. Grant us the ability to accept and share our feelings so that they may be used for the good of ourselves, and of others, and of you. In the name of you, whom Elisabeth tells us is with us always, Amen.

QUESTIONS FOR JOURNALING AND REFLECTION

1. Julian describes the devil in detail. Barbara Crafton translates the psalmist's enemies to be the spirits of sadness and worthlessness. How would you describe the demons that plague you?

2. What are some of the strategies—patience, humor, listening to music, gratitude, anger, painting, long walks, prayer—that have helped you be rid of demons in the past?

3. What have you learned about depression, anxiety, and other troubles, as well as helpful strategies that would be helpful to others? Remind yourself by making a list—and remember to share it with others.

4. Elisabeth went from heaving her psalter across the room to visions so fine they even smelled lovely. Remember a huge contrast in your moods and try to recall how you got from point A to point B. Now, remember what you've learned.

6

SURVIVING MIDDLE AGE WITH YOUR MENTAL HEALTH INTACT

I'm done trying to figure out why I do it. Maybe it's because I honed the habit as a single, working mother. Maybe it's because I've had so many more opportunities than my mother, who, despite her intelligence and adventurous spirit, lived her life in the space of two counties. In any case, I'm still in the habit of trying to do too many things at once. It's only when everything collapses—the sermon is rushed, and sounds it; the bread hasn't risen long enough, and tastes it; I haven't gotten to the gym, and feel it; family and friends feel ignored, and act it—that I come to terms with the fact that although I may be able to multitask, I cannot multi-focus.

Regardless of why I try to do too much at once, I'm learning that when I overload myself with responsibility, real or imagined, I am opening the door to failure, burnout, exhaustion, depression, and anxiety, none of which are exactly good neighbors. When I allow myself to be responsible for everything, I also open the door to attempting to replace God with myself (this is what theologians call "original sin"), which is always a losing proposition. The remedy, I've found, is giving myself permission to concentrate. Doing one thing at a time soothes my anxiety and improves my self-esteem, because I feel better about what I can accomplish. And I'm learning that whatever it takes to promote mental health is worth the effort.

MEDIEVAL MODELS OF MENTAL HEALTH

A common trick a lot of midlife women play on ourselves is to feel, and act, responsible for everything. But Jesus, via Catherine of Siena, doesn't recommend this: "I in my providence did not give to any one person or to each individually the knowledge for doing everything necessary for human life. No, I gave something to one, something else to another, so that each one's need would be a reason to have recourse to the other."[1] In other words, there's a divine plan for us to need each other. So don't go trying to do everything for everybody all at once. Treat your psyche with care—mental illness is *not* in the divine plan for you.

Even Catherine of Siena felt overwhelmed sometimes, and tried to protect herself. Apparently, at least once she did so by retreating to the roof. Some local parents were worried that their baby was possessed by demons, so they set out to ask Catherine for help. When Catherine saw the three on their way to her cottage, she felt so overwhelmed that she hid herself on the roof, muttering all the while, "Alas, every day I am tormented by evil spirits: Do you think I want anybody else's?" On Catherine's less stressful days, she poked fun at the devil, calling him "the Old Pickpocket."[2] Then, as now, the devil could steal enjoyment of life from you—and one of Catherine's strategies to keep him at bay was humor.

Catherine's courage was hard-won. At age sixteen, she became what was called a *mantellata*—although she lived at home, she wore the black and white Dominican habit and dedicated herself to prayer and caring for the ill (two-thirds of Siena's population died of the plague when Catherine was one, and outbreaks continued throughout her life). For the next three years, whenever she was in her room, Catherine experienced an incessant buzzing of demonic voices that questioned her choice. Didn't she know nice girls got married? She'd be sorry if she didn't have children. What did she think she was trying to do? There would be no way to back out of any vows she might make. What difference would it make anyway?

Catherine's strategy (which showed she did indeed know what she was doing in persisting to lead the spiritual life) was to ignore the enemy. Give him your attention, she advised, and he's winning. Instead, she focused her attention on a sort of mantra: "I trust in the Lord Jesus Christ, not in myself."[3] Clearly, Catherine viewed the incessant demands that could lead to depression, anxiety, and mental illness as the work of the devil. And she was determined to remain sane.

If your growing-up years contained trauma (such as Catherine's early loss of her mother, or childhood sexual abuse), it's common to always be on guard. It's hard to trust anything or anyone, including God. It's typical to be beset by a sense that something's going to go wrong any minute now. Even when the fear is leftover from the past, and not rational in the present, fear often wins struggles with security, because the habit is so engrained. My hunch is that Beatrice of Nazareth (c. 1200–1258), who lost her mother as a young child, understood this struggle, because she writes movingly of the fear that "makes one suffer . . . for fear of transitory calamity."[4]

Beatrice seems to understand the power of fear to undermine healing. Jesus, who advises us "Do not fear, only believe" (Mark 5:36) seems to understand this as well. Belief that Jesus can and does heal doesn't come easily to many of us, especially if one's childhood was particularly frightening. But both Jesus and

Beatrice seem to understand that fear can dilute or delay or even block healing.

Ever practical, ever psychologically sound Julian recommends that we lay off our self-blame. She stressed that we often assume God is blaming us when actually we're blaming ourselves. Although sin causes pain, sin is a product of our being imperfect humans.

> *Because of the tender love which our good Lord has for all who will be saved, he comforts readily and sweetly, meaning this: It is true that sin is the cause of all this pain, but all will be well, and every kind of thing will be well. These words were revealed most tenderly, showing no kind of blame to me to anyone who will be saved.*[5]

Here's Julian summary: "As I see it, there is no anger in God."[6] Even though, just down the lane from her cell and, indeed, throughout Europe, people were burned on the grounds of heresy as if to appease an angry god. There is no anger in God! What an extraordinary, even dangerous assertion in Julian's day, and perhaps in our own as well. When was the last time you heard it preached that there is no anger in God?

Catherine of Genoa also campaigned against self-blame, as her sense that life's suffering prepares us for heavenly bliss unfolded.

> *The last ten years of Catherine's life [she lived to be about sixty-three] were marked by violent interior emotions, mentioned in her works. It has been said that in many ways Catherine of Genoa is a "theologian of purgatory," a purgatory that she herself experienced in a marriage she did not desire, in her care for plague victims, and also in her nervous illness. She also experienced purgatory spiri-*

*tuality as the soul's realizations of its own imperfections,
in her search for salvation and purification.*[7]

Not one of our mystics is into self-blame. This may be
common sense in our day, when therapy is fairly commonplace,
but many medievals considered mental suffering a choice, even a
sin. The imaginative punishment to which Dante (1265–1321)
consigns those who commit the sin of *accidie,* or a kind of slug-
gishness and procrastination, reflects the pervasive medieval view
toward depression. "'Joy we denied,' they [the damned souls]
mutter in the mud, 'out there in the sweet air which takes delight
in the sun, secreted smog within. Now, here, under the black,
thick tide we learn all about despair.'"[8]

Our mystics didn't deny the existence of despair, but they
understood that blaming yourself for everything is unhealthy. In
their minds, this habit was probably dangerously close to the
original sin—trying to be God. Those of us who have suffered
childhood abuse may be particularly susceptible to this way of
thinking. As children, it is impossible to understand the world
except in relationship to ourselves, and assuming we caused
everything made sense of the chaos abuse causes. Julian,
especially, was quick to remind us that whether we are feeling
"well being or woe," we express God's love.

*I was changed, and abandoned to myself, oppressed and
weary of my life and ruling myself, so that I hardly had
the patience to go on living. I felt that there was no ease
or comfort for me except faith, hope, and love, and truly
I felt very little of this. And then presently God gave me
again comfort and rest for my soul, delight and security
so blessedly and so powerfully that there was no fear, no
sorrow, no pain, physical or spiritual, that one could
suffer which might have disturbed me. And then again,*

I felt the pain, and then afterwards the delight and the joy, now the one and now the other, again and again, I suppose about twenty times. And in the time of joy I could have said with St. Paul: Nothing shall separate me from the love of Christ; and in the pain I could have said with St. Peter: Lord save me, I am perishing.[9]

Julian knew what she was talking about when she told us that

our Lord freely gives what it is his will to give, and sometimes lets us suffer woe—and both are part of one love. For bliss is lasting and pain is passing, and shall come to nothing for those who shall be saved. . . . it is not God's will that we should linger over pain with sorrow . . . but that we should pass quickly through it to joy without end.[10]

MIDLIFE: DON'T LOSE YOUR MIND OVER IT

A number of mystics found that exercising their intellect was a helpful strategy in coping with the suffering they experienced in worlds that must often have felt constraining and limiting. Although the strategy is just as useful today, it would have been even more difficult to adopt in the Middle Ages. In the first place, the medieval world associated the life of the mind exclusively with men (women were linked to nature, which ranked lower than the mind). In the second place, girls rarely had access to education that matched that of their brothers (of course, many of their brothers were uneducated). And then, as now, wealthier girls and women were more likely to be educated than the poor. A girl's education was most likely vocational, and she was most likely taught by her mother. Daughters of noble families were taught to keep household accounts, to card wool, or to brew ale.

Priests, nuns, and monks were the most likely to be literate, and although there is a tradition of intellectual nuns, particularly in Germany, it's a mistake to assume that all medieval nuns could read or write.[11]

Although the university system began growing rapidly in the thirteenth century (as did Gothic cathedrals, including Notre Dame in Paris and the masterpieces in Reims and Chartres), very few women gained access to higher learning, and even fewer gained access to the professions for which the universities prepared their students. One young woman cross-dressed so she could attend classes at the University of Cracow. In another case, when a professor had to be absent, he appointed his daughter to teach in his place. She had to do so behind a curtain lest her beauty distract the students.

Unless you happened to be a priest, even reading the Bible—that is, if you could read—in private was highly controversial in the Middle Ages. It was also expensive to own any book, especially one as lengthy and as embellished as the Bible. It could even be illegal to indulge in reading the Bible. Like many church officials, Archbishop of Canterbury Thomas Arundell (1353–1414) thought that people reading the Bible for themselves without benefit of explanation by a clergyman was dangerous. He went so far as to forbid laypeople to read the Bible privately, as well as to argue theological issues outside a university.

Birgitta of Sweden tried to skirt this issue a bit when, at around age forty-seven, she began to dedicate her life to church reform. In prayer, she was commanded to study Latin in order to communicate with church officials. She claimed that St. Agnes comforted her when she whined that Latin lessons took time away from her prayer, and that learning Latin was an extremely difficult, odious, and tedious task for an older person in the first place!

HELFTA: A HAVEN FOR THOSE BRAINY GERMANIC TYPES

A shining oasis for women who longed for formal education was often inside a convent, particularly German convents. "The crown of German convents" was Helfta, in a northeastern village not far from Martin's Luther's hometown of Eisleben. In 1251, the convent came under the direction of an amazing woman whose family once owned the property. Gertrude of Hackeborn (1223–1292) became abbess at age nineteen and served until her death forty years later. Helfta's well-stocked library was Gertrude's legacy. At Abbess Gertrude's insistence, Helfta nuns received an education on par with that available in universities, studying grammar, rhetoric, logic, arithmetic, geometry, astronomy, and music. In addition, Helfta nuns studied theology, especially the works of Bernard of Clairvaux, whose view of God was kinder and gentler than predecessors such as Augustine. Although the best-educated nuns taught the novices the university topics, Dominican brothers were the only ones trusted to teach theology and scripture; they also offered spiritual direction. In terms of offering their gifts to the world, of course, even the sisters of Helfta were distinctly disadvantaged in comparison to their equally well-educated male peers who studied at universities.

In its medieval heyday, Helfta was one of the largest convents in Europe, housing over a hundred nuns. During the sixteenth-century Reformation, ignited by Martin Luther (1483–1546), the buildings fell into disrepair and, eventually, the convent became a state farm. In the mid-1990s, however, eighteen nuns returned the convent to its original purpose and two dozen or so use the convent these days, supporting themselves through running a sort of bed and breakfast in its renovated buildings.

One of Helfta's most illustrious alumnae is Gertrude the Great (1256–1302). Apparently, she lost both parents in early childhood and was given to the convent to be raised at age five.

In a tone reminiscent of Lisa Simpson, Gertrude proclaimed, "No man shall surpass me in learnedness." Indeed, they were hard-pressed. Gertrude's scholarship in the sciences, the arts, and theology was unsurpassed. She spoke and wrote Latin and Greek fluently and translated parts of the Bible into German, beating Luther, who appeared over two hundred years later, to the task that helped make him such a hero.

Gertrude the Great seemed to be one of those people who found refuge in her sizeable intellect. Nevertheless, for reasons we can only speculate (were some of the sisters jealous of her?), she was deeply unhappy. She inhabited her mind only, and deemed herself a hypocritical nun, as she ignored her soul. Shortly after her twenty-fifth birthday, everything changed. She reported that God, apparently unbidden and unexpected, dispersed "the darkness of my night." A young man, "handsome and gracious," asked Gertrude gently, "Why are you so sad? Is it because you have no one to confide in that you are sorrowful? . . . I will save you. I will deliver you. Do not fear."[12]

After Gertrude's conversion experience in the middle of her life, she began to hear the voice of her soul in addition to that of her mind. In answer to the questions of why God came to her at that very moment and in the very way that God did, Gertrude said that God has a knack for revealing the Divine Self to us in ways that are as unique as we are. After all, God made us our unique selves in the first place.[13]

Like Gertrude the Great, Hrosvit of Gandersheim (c. 935– c. 973), with her impressive intellect, was fortunate to land where learning was valued. The convent at Gandersheim was, however, less open than Helfta, as only nobles were admitted. Although the sisters took vows of chastity and obedience, Gandersheim was in some ways more like a finishing school than a convent. Servants were allowed, as were visitors, including suitors. You could own property, such as books. While waiting for your family to find you a suitable mate, however, you were expected to study with the impressive teachers and avail yourself of the extensive library. For a woman like Hrosvit, confined by her class and times and with a mind aching to be exercised, the scholarship must have provided life-saving freedom.

Thus, Hrosvit—who never married, by the way—was well schooled in Greek and Roman literature, and her early work consists mostly of retellings of classical legends in her own language. She also wrote histories and hagiographies. But her most interesting works are the plays in which she veers from the classics to portray women as strong and rational instead of as weak and emotional. Playwriting had pretty much been ignored since classical times, and we owe a debt to Hrosvit for picking it up again. She was more than just an imitator, however, as she revealed her own voice—keenly aware of the double standards of her day and unafraid to show off her knowledge. Hrosvit was also a pioneer as a poet, being the first known person to write poetry in what is now Germany.

Hrosvit apparently believed she owed God the use of her talents as a sort of thank-you gift. In a preface to her plays, she wrote,

> *I also know that God has given me a sharp mind, but my mind has remained neglected through my own inertia and untrained ever since the efforts of my teachers ceased to nurture it. Therefore, in order to prevent God's gift in me to die by my neglect, I have tried whenever I could probe, to rip small patches from Philosophy's robe and weave them into this little work of mine, so that the worthlessness of my own ignorance may be ennobled by the interweaving of this nobler material's shine, and that, thus, the Giver of my talent all the more be justly praised through me, the more limited the female intellect is believed to be.*[14]

Hrosvit inspires us to give God all we have. Keep striving to know more, to contribute more—regardless of what you believe your limitations to be.

THE DANGERS OF KNOWING TOO MUCH

Things didn't work out so nicely for Marguerite Porete, who was burned at the stake in Paris in 1310 for heresy. Marguerite's voice came forth in *The Mirror of Simple Souls*, a passionate, lyrical book in which she refers to the soul as "the pearl of God." In writing about higher states of the soul (Marguerite saw seven—the highest achievable only in eternity), she declared, "And so this Soul is like the eagle, because this Soul flies high, indeed, very high, higher than any other bird because she is feathered by Fine Love. She sees more clearly the beauty of the sun, the rays of the sun, and the splendour of the sun, and the rays which feed her with the marrow of the high cedars."[15] Marguerite's assertion that the soul is beloved, wildly free, and can be a "she" got her in deep trouble. (I wonder how many envied Marguerite's deftly beautiful writing style.)

Possibly, Marguerite was a Beguine, though she writes that they, a varied group, to be sure, were among her critics. She may have been an early member of the Brethren of Free Spirit movement, which shunned authority (like the pope) and boldly claimed God's presence everywhere.

Regardless of the circumstances, a historian sums up the sad story of Marguerite thusly: "Her crime, then, was that she insisted on speaking publicly, teaching her ideas publicly, and that she did so in her own voice."[16] A sort of freelance writer, Marguerite spoke only for her own soul. And she died for speaking in her own voice. So recall Marguerite's bravery next time you lack courage to speak the truth of *your* life.

Hildegard, certainly among the most outrageous of our mystics, was no less respectful of the pope than Marguerite, and she certainly found God everywhere, but as a Benedictine, she was part of the religious system *and* she wisely claimed that, as a prophet, she was speaking on someone else's—God's—behalf. Though unquestionably shrewd, Hildegard often referred to her rudimentary education with regret. The Latin Hildegard was taught to read and write by Jutta, the nun who raised her, was pretty much the extent of her education. Despite Hildegard's regrets, I wonder if being unable to devote herself to scholarship allowed Hildegard time for creative endeavors.

Musician-priest Victoria R. Sirota points out that because Hildegard was not restrained, as a classically trained composer might have been, she was free to innovate so that her music and theology are welded as one. For instance, in Hildegard's morality play, *Ordo Virtutum* (*Order of the Virtues*), "the devil cannot sing. What a simple but brilliant theological and dramatic decision. Evil is overcome by good through love. The devil's spoken empty threats and half truths are answered by melodic phrases which do not lose their identity in anger or fear."[17]

Although Hildegard's eighty surviving compositions are not the earliest musical works we have in the West, "Hildegard von Bingen" is the first composer's name we have attached to music in the western world. It's fitting that Hildegard is still recognized as a creative genius, since her passion would not be quelled. When Hildegard was abbess and the convent was punished for allowing the burial of a man who had been excommunicated, she told the bishop off. The punishment included denial of the Eucharist, but it was the prohibition against music that enraged Hildegard into warning the bishop, "Those who choose to silence music in this lifetime will go to a place where they will be without the company of the angelic song of praises on heaven." What's more, Hildegard wrote to tell the bishop where she thought he'd spend eternity at age eighty, a year before her death (the interdict was lifted in the nick of time), proving that she was engaged in life all her life long.

Staying Engaged, Staying Sane

A former parishioner of mine, Ruth, reminds me a little of Hildegard, because aging is her excuse to further engage with the world. When I asked her about the experience of earning a master's degree after raising seven kids, Ruth asked me, "The one in women's history I started when I was sixty-five, or the one in creative writing I've just started?" Ruth is in her early eighties, old enough to be my mother, and clearly, I have a hard time keeping up with her. In answer to why she started grad school to earn a degree in sixteenth-century women's history at an age when most people are retiring, Ruth said, "Well, I always wanted to earn a master's degree in history, sort of like a man who always wanted a fancy car." This second master's degree, though, reflects that as much as Ruth enjoyed caring for her children and working in journalism, she realizes that "I spent my life taking care of other people, writing words for other people, helping other people tell their stories," and now, "You know, when you know you don't have a lot of time left, you sort of lose patience. The big question becomes 'How do I want to spend the time I have left?' I don't have time to spend on people who are boring me, and I certainly don't want to bore myself. I don't think you have to go to college to do it—for me, earning a degree gives me discipline—but the point is you can never afford to be closed to learning. It's mandatory to exercise your mind, to be creative, to be interested in the world. Otherwise, you'll grow old far less happily."

The other day, I saw a piece on television about a woman who has broken into modeling in her seventies. She's always been a sort of fitness freak, of course, eats wisely, sleeps well, and is blessed with good genes, but, most importantly, she refused to give up her dream. Having raised three children and run a business with her husband, now she glories in doing what she wants to do. "The best part," she gushed, as a makeup artist fussed over her, "is that now people are doing things for *me!*"

Which goes to show that it's never worth giving up your dreams. So don't. And do use your mind, your creativity, and every gift God has ever given you. When dreams come true, and even when new dreams emerge, it's mystical evidence that the divine is longing for us to give over our sorrow. That's worth remembering when you're feeling depressed, confused, anxious, or fearful—and not bad to remember when you're feeling happy, either.

A PRAYER TO GET STARTED

God who has given us brains as well as hearts: Thank you for the gift of our intellect, which the Helfta nuns remind us is so potent. Thank you for the gifts of our hearts, which Julian reveals are so wise. Give us ears to hear the stories of those like Marguerite who inspire us. Open our eyes as you did Catherine of Siena's, to see life's infinite possibilities. Help us, like Julian, avoid the bitter taste of self-blame. Make us grateful for all the resources—friends, professionals, stories, ideas, creativity—you give us to claim your gift of resilience. In the name of you, whom Julian reminds us contains no anger, Amen.

Questions for Journaling and Reflection

1. Remember the story of Mary and Martha of Bethany (Luke 10:38–42)? When Jesus visited them in Bethany, Mary stayed with the men and listened to Jesus' teaching while Martha busied herself with preparing the meal. Many Christians have used the personalities of these two women to teach us the importance of both reflection (Mary) and action (Martha). How much balance is in your life? And how important is balance to you?

2. When you read the story of my friend Ruth and her assertion that "when you know you don't have a lot of time left, you sort of lose patience. The big question becomes 'How do I want to spend the time I have left?'"—what did you think? How patient or impatient are you feeling these days? And what do you want to accomplish during the rest of your life?

3. I was once advised that I had to experience the pain of losing my husband so I could fully appreciate the happy events of life, which wasn't very comforting, to say the least. I was reminded of this well-intended advice when I read that Julian, a much wiser soul to be sure, asserted that bliss and sorrow belong to the same love. What do you think about the relationship between sorrow and bliss? How has their interplay changed throughout your life?

4. A simple suggestion: Get a CD of Hildegard's music and let it wash over you. Open your spirit to it, and notice what you feel via the music of a woman who lived nine hundred years ago.

7

SAY A LITTLE PRAYER FOR YOU

Has anybody sent you an e-mail notice that you can help fund mammograms with the click of your mouse? Companies that advertise on www.thebreastcancersite.com donate money for mammograms each time you click (and presumably look at their ads). Once you click for mammograms, you'll notice tabs to click on sites that promote the feeding of stray animals, teach disabled children to walk, and other good causes.

Taking the lead from Teresa of Avila (1515–1582), who explains that the first step of prayer is to collect one's thoughts, rather like bees returning to their hive,[1] I allow my morning clicks to structure my fuzzy morning brain into prayer. I click on the breast cancer site and pray for the ill, click on the hunger site and pray for the hungry, click on the child health site and pray for the young and the elderly, click on the literacy site and pray for the ignorant, click on the rain forest site and pray for the earth, click on the animal rescue site and pray for the vulnerable. Because the clicking is truly beneficial (on a recent day, 1,741 books were donated to needy kids through the literacy site), this simple exercise focuses my mind, connects me to God and others, and does some good in the world.

As a priest, I sometimes have the privilege of listening to folks describe their experiences of the divine, and more than once I've been told of feeling God through the senses. When my husband was dying of cancer, both of us began to feel a warming sensation between our shoulders as we prayed, as if a hand of love were on us. In Psalm 139, the psalmist writes joyfully of God's inescapable love, praising God for "lay[ing] your hand upon me." And maybe we Christians shouldn't be so surprised when we experience God's love through our bodies; after all, for us, God expresses the ultimate love in the human body of Christ. (For the record, theologians call this "incarnational theology.")

The need to communicate with God is simply part of being human. As author Philip Zaleski puts it,

> *prayer is something essential to our nature, as if it were hardwired in us. It's something that we need to do, and something that feels good when we do it. Even in the midst of suffering, prayer is, if not a release from suffering, a way to find meaning in suffering. So, prayer always helps in some way or other. It fulfills something in us that we need to have fulfilled. It seems as natural as drinking, or eating, or sleeping, or talking.*[2]

Yet, praying is not always easy. This may have something to do with our society—in which prayer is defined, as it was by a recent *New York Times* crossword puzzle clue, as "bows one's head in church." While I'm a big fan of crosswords, and of the ones in the *Times* in particular, and I understand that they're a game, I think this clue opens a window onto a prevalent attitude, one in which prayer is nothing more than a quaint posture, a relic of other times and places. For medieval Europeans, though, it was nearly impossible to ignore prayer. As observant Muslims have always done, they stopped throughout the day to pray. Throughout Christendom, in villages as well as in cities, church bells were rung at dawn, noon, and sunset, and peasant and prince alike would pause to cross themselves, bow their heads, and pray. Some would say the rosary then, unknowingly borrowing the practice of praying with beads from the Eastern Hindus, Buddhists, and Muslims.

Even today, some people find that simply fingering their prayer beads helps them begin to pray. I feel that way when I get on my bicycle and know that my feet will soon carry me into exercise; my musically inclined friend says she feels that way when she sits down at the piano and allows her fingers to practice.

Honing the habit of prayer is also like being a mother with kids at home and wanting to sleep in. But it's a school day, lunches must be packed, and the baby's stirring down the hall. So you get up and change the baby cheerfully, help your third-grader find his homework, and assure your kindergartener that everything will be all right on the field trip. Though you don't feel like doing any of these things, you do them out of love. So it is with prayer. Sometimes you just have to push yourself, having faith that what you're doing makes a difference (as it was when you read to your children every day, played Legos® with them, and packed healthy lunches). Above all, Teresa advised, "We . . . should not abandon prayer, which is what the devil wants us to do. For the most part all the trials and disturbances come from our not understanding ourselves."[3]

TERESA OF AVILA: A PRAYER-DRENCHED LIFE

For Teresa of Avila, prayer offered the freedom to concentrate and the liberty to avoid competing demands. She never claimed getting started was easy, however; she compared beginning to pray to carrying a bucket of water on your shoulders from a distant well.

Teresa's life wasn't easy, though she remained feisty through it all. She is said to have prayed, "God protect me from gloomy saints"—and she certainly didn't become a "gloomy saint" herself. On her way to enter the convent, Teresa supposedly exposed her ankles and advised, "Take a good look, boys—you won't be seeing these again." She entered religious life against her family's wishes. On her father's side, she was descended from *conversos*, Jews who were forced to convert to Christianity during the Spanish Inquisition, a reality of Spanish life from 1478 until the early nineteenth century. Although there's no indication that Teresa's family—she was one of ten children—maintained their Judaism in secret, as some *conversos* did, neither did they want her to be a nun. Her resolve strengthened by her reading of St. Jerome and perhaps by the loss of her mother when she was a young teenager, Teresa disobeyed her father and entered the Carmelite Monastery of the Incarnation in her hometown of Avila. Two years later, she took vows as Teresa of Jesus.

Things didn't go well in the convent, as Teresa took ill shortly after entering, even falling into a coma, and spent three of her early years there partially paralyzed. She found that she prayed long and deep while she was ill, but let prayer go when she was well. Incarnation was so poor that although the nuns were supposed to live completely enclosed, they sometimes had to leave the convent to return home for food and medical care. Teresa left three times—once while ill, once to care for her dying father, and once to go on pilgrimage to a Spanish shrine. If Teresa had entered the convent expecting to live in a self-sufficient community, she was disappointed. Visitors had to be welcomed, and charmed, because each was a potential donor.

As with so many of us, Teresa didn't really come into her own until midlife. At forty, she had her first vision of Christ, and as soon as she shared that she was experiencing Christ in a more real way than ever before, she received a volley of advice. Most agreed that she was far too flaky to be chosen by Jesus, and that the visions were actually the work of the devil. One priest even advised her to make the sign of the cross and laugh at her visions. Like Julian, Teresa seemed to know when a vision was of the devil or of God, and so she knew when to laugh. And she had the last laugh, because nowadays, Teresa is the patron saint of those who are ridiculed for their piety.

Teresa's visions convinced her to build a new monastery that was truer to the original ideal of her religious order. At age forty-five, she embarked on her building project. Though she had no preparation for such an undertaking, Teresa knew what she wanted: a place where enclosure meant enclosure—no trips into town for parties or socializing, and no social visitors. The nuns' lives were to be dedicated to prayer and study. Understanding that cluttered environments invite cluttered minds, Teresa insisted that convent life be pared down to necessities, and prayer was necessity number one. Originally, Carmelite nuns were to be "discalced," that is, without shoes, as a symbol of their poverty. Teresa's reforms included sandals only. Simplicity of life, she maintained, makes prayer easier.

The resistance to Teresa's dream of building a new, reformed convent didn't win her any friends at Incarnation. Having secured the funds from church authorities (whose support wavered as they were pressured by town authorities), Teresa knew she didn't have time to waste. Her ingenious solution was to ask a sister and brother-in-law to live in the house and pretend to be settling in even as it was being remodeled into a convent under the town's collective nose. Neither Teresa's dedication to reforming the Carmelite Order (she kept her promise of living by vows that were even stricter than the ones she imposed), nor her persistence in prayer, nor her personal charm can be underestimated. Facing down lawsuits from neighbors who resisted convents in their neighborhood as well as church authorities, Teresa persisted, received the papal blessing (fully documented in writing, of course—Teresa was nobody's fool), and eventually founded fifteen monasteries of Carmelites of the Reformed Observance, including two for men. Her followers founded two more.

Like any entrepreneur, Teresa found that expansion brought new challenges. During the first five years after leaving Incarnation, Teresa was completely accessible to the sisters with whom she lived at the first convent she established, St. Joseph's of Avila. Over time, she established monasteries as far north as Burgos and as far south as Granada. Given that Teresa's plate was full with founding convents, and that travel in those days was slow and arduous, it could be years before Teresa was available to answer questions in person. Having completed her autobiography at St. Joseph's, Teresa took up the pen again when she began her expansion plan at age fifty-two. *The Way of Perfection*, which placed Teresa in the role of spiritual cheerleader for her nuns, was completed shortly before she established her second convent. The remainder of her life was dedicated to founding monasteries and to writing—hymns, prayers, and letters, over 450 of which still exist. *Foundations*, which was eleven years in the making and the last book Teresa completed, is a history of the order. Her penultimate work, *The Interior Castle*, which she completed at age sixty-five, is Teresa's masterpiece. Because *The Interior Castle* is about prayer, it speaks most directly to us today.

Teresa was suspect for many reasons—she was a woman, she was a reformer (which means she was a whistleblower), and she was a visionary who experienced Christ in mystical ways. Working and writing as she did during the Spanish Inquisition (and with Jewish heritage to boot), Teresa was under constant scrutiny. But because of the Inquisition, Teresa's work was read by many powerful clergy (whose power in sixteenth-century Spain cannot be underestimated), and, as it was circulated, both she and her ideas became ironically famous. An indication of Teresa's popularity is that although the name Teresa was among the most common names for baby girls in Spain and Portugal when Teresa was born in 1515, it was rarely heard outside the Iberian Peninsula until her fame popularized the name via Austria, whose royal family was related to Spanish nobility. And so the name Teresa swept through Europe and even across the oceans and the centuries. Teresa was on the fast track to sainthood; she was beatified a mere thirty-two years after her death, and canonized only eight years later. In 1970, she and Catherine of Siena were proclaimed "Doctors of the Church" by the Roman Catholic Church. The only other woman among the thirty-three doctors is Thérèse of Lisieux (1873–1897), who, like "our" Teresa, was a Carmelite.

Neither scrutiny nor age slowed Teresa of Avila down; she founded her last four convents in the last three years of her life. While traipsing through Spain to check on her convents, Teresa became ill and died at age sixty-seven.

Teresa's legacy to us includes a richly conveyed understanding of prayer. Thank goodness for a spiritual director who pushed her to write when she protested, "Let the learned men do the writing and leave me to my spinning." Teresa managed to create metaphors that leave our heads nodding in agreement while warning us that no two of us ever walks the same path. Yet most of us can understand Teresa's experience of getting started in prayer as difficult and as unappealing as hoisting heavy buckets of sloshing water on our shoulders. Once we get started praying, though, Teresa claimed it begins to feel as if the pump were carrying the water to us. We start to realize that the very nature of prayer is that we're not alone.

Yet, Teresa said, this more relaxed state is often followed by a period of dryness, when you don't feel yourself in relation to God. Tears are often the remedy, according to Teresa, because we feel God through our emotions.

PRAYING WOMEN IN MEDIEVAL TIMES

Historians have long characterized the Middle Ages as a time when people, perhaps rebelling against the Greeks and Romans, valued passion—in all aspects of life, including spirituality. Scholar Elizabeth Dreyer describes the era as "a time of intense longing, fierce passion and ardent desire."[4] If there was ever a woman born in the right place and time, it was the endlessly emotive Margery Kempe. Although her prayer would start in a rush of words, over time, it gave way to communicating with God without words. (Sometimes she even fell asleep while praying and claimed she continued praying in her dreams.) Margery experienced God as musical sounds beyond her earthly ears, as sights beyond her earthly eyes, as scents beyond her earthly nose. Fellow medieval mystic Richard Rolle (1290–1349) of Hampole, England, felt God warm his body. He wrote of his initial encounter with God in this way:

> *I cannot tell you how surprised I was the first time I felt my heart begin to warm. It was real warmth, too, not imaginary, and it felt as if it were actually on fire. I was astonished at the way the heat surged up, and how this new sensation brought great and unexpected comfort. I had to keep feeling my breast to make sure there was no physical reason for it! But once I realized that it came entirely from within . . . I was absolutely delighted, and wanted my love to be even greater.*[5]

As Julian expert Sheila Upjohn, who actually lives about a mile from Julian's cell in Norwich, points out, Julian and Teresa are frequently on the same prayer wavelength,[6] although they could not possibly have known each other. Teresa was born nearly two centuries after Julian, and there is no indication of Spanish Teresa being familiar with English Julian's manuscripts, which, so far as we know, never made it to Spain. Yet Julian's advice on prayer is very similar to Teresa's: "When the soul is tempest-tossed, troubled and cut off by worries," Julian wrote, "then is the time to pray . . . and all our troubles come because our own love fails us."[7]

Teresa's persistence is all the more inspirational when you take into account that she suffered for years at a time from aridity of the soul, or "that great dryness." It was only after nearly twenty years of such dryness that Teresa recognized that there is a hidden river, or pump, bringing God's love to us—there's no need to struggle under the buckets after all. In the next stage of her life, Teresa felt God's love pouring on her like a downpour of rain.

A story Teresa told in her autobiography indicates just how familiar she became with the divine. When Teresa became at ease with her frequent visions of Jesus as well as with talking about them, the sisters asked her to check out the color of Jesus' eyes. When she did so, Jesus got piqued and cut the visit short.

In general, our mystics didn't give us recipes for prayer. They did, however, give us wonderful replays of their conversations with God. Remember when God, "the Living Light," told Hildegard to stop keeping her visions to herself? Much of Mechthild of Magdeburg's book, *The Flowing Light of the Godhead*, are dialogues between God and the soul. And Julian's *Revelations of Divine Love* could be accurately described as an extensive report of her talks with Jesus. Teresa told her nuns that a fruit of being in community is the ability to chat easily with the divine in prayer.

Though our mystics did not tell us how to pray, they certainly weren't shy about telling us to do so. As John Kirvan points out, Teresa's answer to all the difficulties she faced

> *is prayer—prayer when it seems impossible, prayer when others do everything to dissuade you and shake your confidence in it, prayer when you are not sure whether you are being led by God or by a devil. For everyone who told Teresa that she was being blessed by God, there was someone with equal authority telling her that her experiences were the work of Satan. But she never stopped praying.*[8]

Our mystics embraced constant prayer, which went beyond listing what they wanted. Instead of viewing God as a sort of divine Santa Claus to whom they occasionally presented a list of requests, our mystics viewed God as a divine friend. Catherine of Siena went even further; she experienced being joined in a mystical union to Christ in marriage.

PRAYER, THEN AND NOW

In the eight months and four days of my husband's cancer diagnosis, which took him at age thirty-two, I certainly logged my share of prayers of petition. "Oh God, let the diagnosis be wrong." "Please let the chemotherapy work." "Don't let him die." I don't believe God condemned or ignored me for my Christmas-list prayer; I believe God accompanied me, comforted me, and listened to me. But I also believe that God led me, in my deep anxiety and sorrow, to a less specific way of praying. Sometimes even my dreams were prayer. Perhaps influenced by using a cash machine at the hospital that was located at the end of long, white hall, I had a dream one night that the Virgin Mary was in such a hall, waiting for me and telling me to "take the saints to the Protestants."

While the church my family regularly attended while I was growing up was marked by a strong preaching tradition, the saints were never mentioned—though I do have a vague memory of a rather unpopular minister mentioning the Virgin Mary during a Mothers' Day sermon one year, we pretty much stuck to Jesus. It was perhaps out of desperation that when the cancer came, my interest in Mary flowered, and yet I never felt judged for the timing or intensity of my interest in her—I sensed welcome from every member of the communion of saints on whom I called.

When I got the chance several years later to write and produce a video series called *Pioneers of the Spirit*, I knew it was the job for me. These days, I experience the same sense of grounding when I teach, preach, lead retreats, or write about the mystics and their contribution to our faith lives.

Though it has rarely led me to something as concrete as directions from the Virgin Mary, even now, prayer on this deep, satisfying level typically begins with my trying to give to God whatever I'm feeling and whatever the circumstances are. (Notice that I did not say anything about giving God a wish list.) This is hard for me, and sometimes I visualize hands reaching across an altar to take from me whatever it is—being treated unfairly, a sense of inadequacy left over from my childhood, worry about my son's future. This is not to say that I'm unlikely to retrieve whatever I've given. Thankfully, God never goes out of town, so I always feel welcome in repeating these offerings.

In spite of my very human behavior, I've learned that opening myself to the divine connects me to the love that meets all my needs. I wasn't asking for a direction in my life when I dreamed of the Virgin Mary in that tunnel, but the sense of direction has helped sustain me in all that Scott's death has brought. I didn't know what I needed, and yet it has been given to me. There's really no need to treat God like Santa, since, as we're reminded in Matthew 6:8, God knows what we need before we ask.

Teresa also received what she needed without praying for it specifically. Apparently, she didn't realize how hindered she was by her need to be recognized, but over time, as she entered more deeply into relationship with God (and spent less time trying to stuff the divine into a Santa suit), Teresa's desire for praise faded. This is what can happen when we pray for the sake of growing closer to God and opening ourselves to God's will for us. Teresa has taught me how the need to be appreciated can get in the way of achieving what God wants us to. I've often been guilty of chasing prestige, of craving recognition. And when, following Teresa's example, I lift the feelings to God, I find it easier to pursue what's healthier for me and more beneficial for the world in which I am a pilgrim.

Christian Europeans in the Middle Ages frequently used Jesus' physical wounds as a way to pray about their own wounds of all kinds. Perhaps because suffering—plague, poverty, war, hunger, death, and disease—was so common in the Middle Ages, many Christians found meaning in Christ's suffering. Years ago, an older woman who is also a survivor of childhood sexual abuse advised me to "meditate on your wounds," teaching me that coming to terms with the pain could be transforming if, in meditation, I could let my wounds melt into Christ's. This is a very medieval idea, that Christ's passion is an event that transcends history. Medieval people didn't shy away from Christ's suffering—Julian's detailed visions are very graphic, even gruesome by our standards—but it was out of the realization that empathy with another's suffering (especially when the sufferer is God in human flesh) is a healing endeavor.

At a recent exhibition at the Getty Center in Los Angeles, a curator wrote about Simon Bening's painting "The Flagellation," which dates from about 1525–1530:

> *The martyrdom of saints, the torments of hell, and the suffering of Christ were all popular subjects in medieval art. Vivid images of pain reminded the faithful that Christ's suffering was essential to the possibility of salvation. In this flagellation scene, rivulets of blood flow down Christ's body as he is mercilessly whipped by four men. His serene white face contrasts with the goblin-like features of his four torturers. This image is accompanied by a prayer addressed directly to Jesus. The picture and prayer encouraged readers to share in Christ's agony. Like the other works in this exhibition ["Images of Violence in the Medieval World"] this image was designed to have a powerful emotional impact on the viewer.*[9]

Clare reminded us that Christ is more important than his wounds (and maybe so are we). In a letter to Agnes of Prague, a leader among the sisters of what is now the Czech Republic, she wrote a sort of poem that advises us to find both ourselves and our God through contemplating Christ:

> *Place your mind before the mirror of eternity!*
> *Place your soul in the brilliance of glory!*
> *Place your heart in the figure of the divine substance!*
> *And transform your entire being into the image of the Godhead*
>   *Itself through contemplation.*[10]

Did you catch the word "mirror"? Clare is telling us that Christ's humanity is absolutely the most perfect. So to meditate on what is eternally life giving in Christ helps pare away the sin that makes us so imperfect. As Carol Lee Flinders explains,

When we look as closely at the image of Christ as the depth of our own prayer will permit us, we will be looking also at our own real selves. The purpose of contemplative prayer, then, is to draw as close as we can to God incarnate so that ultimately we can discover our own unity with God—not to make ourselves one with God, though we may feel along the way as if we are doing that, but to discover that we have never been anything else.[11]

We Christians believe that as God dwells in Christ, so Christ dwells in us. As Jesus reminds us in the Gospel of John, "Abide in me as I abide in you. . . . Those who abide in me and I in them bear much fruit" (John 15:4–5). This is the simple truth our mystics keep leading us to: that we are so enormously, completely, deeply loved that the Divine chooses to live in us.

Distracted by the responsibilities of this world, answering e-mails and meeting deadlines and planning for retirement and responding to children and parents who are aging simultaneously, this may be the biggest reason we need to pray—to be reminded that we're loved so much that Jesus dwells in each of us. Sometimes, like Margery and Richard and even my late husband and me, you may even feel this love dwelling in your body. After all, Julian wrote that Jesus' thirst for us "will persist in him so long as we are in need, and will draw us up into his bliss."[12] And Teresa encouraged us to continue striving to love God back regardless of the circumstances: "[I]f you should at times fall, don't become discouraged and striving to advance, for even from this fall God will draw out good."[13]

Especially if you're feeling discouraged in your prayer life, you might find a couple of tried and true methods helpful. One is called centering prayer, which traces its roots to the Middle Ages' emphasis on contemplative prayer, or prayer that relies more on intuition than on reason.[14] Simply choose a sacred word such as God, peace, Jesus, light, hope, or even the name of your favorite medieval mystic. Repeat the word gently in your mind over a period of several minutes. Whenever your thoughts stray, gently return to the word. I like to use the analogy of bringing a puppy in paper training back to the task at hand when trying to curb my wandering mind.

If you're drawn to something more structured, there's always the rosary (even Anglicans embrace prayer beads these days). Or there's disciplined reading of scripture prayerfully, such as the form called *lectio divina* (meaning "sacred reading"). In the Episcopal Church's Book of Common Prayer, you can find Morning Prayer, Noonday Prayer, Evening Prayer, and Compline (coming from the Latin for "complete," as in completion of the day). Whether you pray by yourself or with others, there's something very powerful in knowing that you are joining other faithful people by praying at fixed times during the day. You're also linking yourself to a tradition among faithful people that was in place well before Jesus' day.

So, fellow sojourners, navigating your way through the thistles and thickets of middle age, it's easier when you know that Jesus loves you. So know it all the time. At the doctor's office; in the car, late to work *again*; looking down on your bedridden father and realizing that the last time you two shared this vantage point, he was peering into your crib; on the phone, leaving yet another message for your fledging adult of a child. Remember that praying helps you realize the love of God better—which can lead to all kinds of good things, for yourself and for everyone else who shares this world with you.

A PRAYER TO GET STARTED

O God, who is present whether we pray or not, thank you for your presence. Thank you for awaiting our prayer, and for drawing us to you in the meantime. Remind us that we are not alone in our attempts to pray. Remind us that you want us to pray, and that you don't care how we do so. Remind us that you'll take anything we hurl in prayer. Lead us in our meditation on you so that we find you in us and us in you. Give us courage to allow our prayer to be where you take us. In the name of you, whom Teresa reminded us is always eager to have a conversation, Amen.

QUESTIONS FOR JOURNALING AND REFLECTION

1. Studying our mystics has changed my prayer life from being reasonably disciplined (relying mostly on Morning and Evening Prayer in the Book of Common Prayer) to engaging in a constant talk with Jesus. My move toward a more talkative spirituality is a big shift for me, and while the fruits of fixed-time prayer are evident in the solidity of virtually everyone I've ever met who prays in this time-tested way, I'm enjoying the closeness I feel with Jesus in the everyday moments of my life. What shifts has your prayer life taken, and what have they meant for you?

2. In *The Interior Castle*, Teresa described the soul as a castle surrounded by snakes, lizards, and other deterrents. Once you get inside the castle, which is as beautiful and rare as a diamond, there are many lovely rooms with the central room—a sort of holy of holies emanating light—the place where the soul is at one with God. How would you describe your soul? What is it like now, and what would you like it to become?

3. Mechthild of Magdeburg claimed that "God has enough of all things, only to touch the soul is never enough for God." If God's longing for your soul never ends, what is the eternal longing of your soul?[15] To be loved? To be appreciated? To be yourself? Maybe there are many eternal longings in your soul, and prayer can lead you to a

deeper knowledge of them.

4. Consider the following reminder from Teresa:

Christ has no body now but yours
No hands, no feet on earth but yours
Yours are the eyes through which He looks
with compassion on this world
Christ has no body now on earth but yours[16]

Does this make you feel overwhelmed? Abandoned? Empowered? What would happen if you took these feelings to God in prayer?

8

SEX AND/OR MARRIAGE— OR NOT

---

†

One of the most provocative questions I've ever been asked came from one of the sweetest-looking ladies I've ever seen, with a silvery blue, tightly coiffed head: "When those mystics talk about these experiences with Christ, aren't they just trying to describe an orgasm?" Maybe. But it's important to remember that Christ as a bridegroom was a potent medieval image. Interestingly, the Hindus speak of a similar impulse called "bridal mysticism," or an intense longing to be one with the divine—a desire the mystics certainly experienced.

When our mystics proclaimed their love for Christ, they refused to hide their adoration. They insisted there's nothing secretive about loving Jesus above all others—faith is no need for shame or embarrassment. And the reminder from the Middle Ages that Jesus walked this earth as we do, sweating, bleeding, weeping—helps us know that he welcomes us as a friend—even if the idea of Jesus as boyfriend makes us feel pretty uncomfortable.

But think of it this way: the human heart is made to love. It's hard to argue with Catherine of Siena, who said, "The human heart is drawn by love as by nothing else, since it is made of love. This seems to be why human beings love so much, because they are made of nothing but love, body and soul."[1] Of course, that always set us up for tremendous complications—from deep satisfaction to broken hearts of all varieties—as it always has and always will. Margery of Kempe writes about being tempted to indulge in an affair and ends up being grateful for having narrowly avoided it. Attitudes toward adultery, sexuality, and commitment have shifted enormously since the Middle Ages, and I suspect there is a wider variety of attitudes toward sexuality in our own day. A gulf between medieval views of sexuality and marriage and our own is no wonder. Birth control and childbirth were much riskier endeavors then, medieval Christians valued asceticism (including fasting and celibacy) more highly than we tend to, and the concept of sexual suppression hadn't been invented. I've uncovered nary a mention of same-sex marriage or sex-reassignment surgery in the Middle Ages, but the descriptions of the giddiness of falling in love and the agonies of broken hearts read as if they were written yesterday.

Still I think our mystics would sympathize with the complicated nature of marriage today. Whether middle age brings with it milestone anniversaries, divorce, death, encore marriages, sexuality shifts, or any combination of the above, no one denies it's complicated—as was marriage and all relating to it in the Middle Ages as well. Marriages among the wealthy were frequently more about political alliances and land acquisition than about anything else. In general, girls were deemed ready to marry at twelve, boys at fourteen, though betrothals, especially to foster political ties, often occurred in infancy. In the twelfth century, some forward-thinking bishops insisted no one be betrothed prior to age seven, but marriage remained a fact of teen life throughout the Middle Ages. Witness Princess Joan of England, who died of the plague in 1348 at age fifteen while on her way to Spain to marry a prince she'd never met.

In *Grown-Up Marriage*, writer Judith Viorst, whose work chronicles contemporary middle age, sets forth a view of marriage for today's midlife women that would ring as true with medieval women as it does today—until the last sentence. "We married because, for a woman, there was no higher attainment," she writes. "And we married to be taken care of financially. We also married in order to have safe sex, which—had we been pressed—we would have defined as sex that wouldn't make getting pregnant a vast catastrophe. We also—most of us—married to get pregnant and raise a family. Of course what we said was that we married for love."[2]

LOVE, SEX, AND MARRIAGE IN THE MIDDLE AGES

Although there were plenty of medieval women in love with their husbands, they weren't as likely as we to say they were marrying for love. As church historian Mary Hope Griffin puts it, "I'm not sure that there was ever a time when marriage was loveless. The shift is from the idea that love comes after marriage into the modern notion that you marry because you are already in love."[3]

It was around the eleventh century that "courtly love" began, in the courts of Europe's royals—especially in what is now France. This movement was a sort of formalization of flirting (and sometimes beyond) that was designed to flatter both ladies and knights. In the poetry of courtly love—written in the language of the people instead of in Latin, the language of the church and the court—women caused their suitors to become pale and lovesick, too weakened by the women's wiles to resist temptation—mirroring the story of Adam and Eve.

Over time, courtly love sometimes encompassed marriage

(and enough hanky panky that it's been labeled a "culture of adultery"[4]), but the expectation that marriage among the nobility could, and even should, include love slowly began to have as much weight as political allegiances. (The peasants, with less power to lose and to gain, understood this concept long before the nobility.)

The marriage of Eleanor of Aquitaine to Henry II of France in 1152 is notable because the pair is credited for being the first royal couple to have chosen each other. The union was also notable because Eleanor was eleven years her groom's senior, had insisted on a divorce from Louis VII of France, had won a legal battle returning her premarital lands, and had given custody of her children to their father. Although whispers of adultery swirled around the couple, they were powerful enough to deflect the accusations.

Eleanor's fellow medieval women faced harsh sentences for adultery, although details varied from region to region and over time. If a woman was unfaithful in thirteenth-century Spain, her husband or fiancé could kill her and her lover without punishment. Adulterous women in parts of fourteenth-century Italy were flogged through the streets prior to their exile. In general, peasant husbands were encouraged to beat straying wives. If her lover had a bit of money or land, the wronged husband was entitled to that as well, in addition to being allowed to beat his wife. In some cases, adulterous women were exiled.

An aside into our own time: shamefully, domestic abuse continues to flourish. The Family Violence Prevention Fund reports that estimates range from 960,000 incidents of violence against a current or former spouse, boyfriend, or girlfriend,[5] to three million women who are physically abused by their husbands or boyfriends per year.[6] If *you* are being threatened or harmed in any way, get help. Right now. Call the National Domestic Violence Hotline at 1-800-799-SAFE (7233) or TTY

1-800-787-3224. You deserve to be safe (and so do your children and grandchildren). And you also have a place in my prayers.

The biggest difference between medieval and modern wife battering is that it was more acceptable and therefore less shameful for medieval husbands. There are many examples of how domestic abuse of women was condoned throughout Europe in the Middle Ages. From France's thirteenth-century French legal code *Customs of Beauvais* (from the birthplace of courtly love!): "In a number of cases men may be excused for the injuries they inflict on their wives, nor should the law intervene. Provided he neither kills nor maims her, it is legal for a man to beat his wife when she wrongs him." A Florentine axiom went: "A good woman and a bad one equally require the stick." And fifteenth-century Siena's *Rules of a Marriage* directed husbands,

> *When you see your wife commit an offense, don't rush at her with insults and violent blows: rather, first correct the wrong lovingly and pleasantly, and sweetly teach her not to do it again. . . . But if your wife is of a servile disposition and has a crude and shifty spirit, so that pleasant words have no effect, scold her sharply, bully, and terrify her. And if this still doesn't work . . . take up a stick and beat her soundly . . . not in rage, but out of charity and concern for soul."*[7]

The idea of a husband's ownership of his wife ran so deep that Margery of Kempe ran into trouble when she traveled from her home in Norfolk to York without written permission from her husband.

In general, divorce—even in the case of domestic abuse—was unheard of in the Middle Ages except in extreme cases, such as a blood relationship unknown prior to marriage. Henry VIII borrowed this argument in 1533, when he insisted that his marriage to Catherine of Aragon be annulled, arguing that his marriage to Catherine was incestuous because she had been married to his late brother, which should therefore have freed him to marry Anne Boleyn—which he did. When Protestants like Luther and Calvin came along, they said cuckolded men could divorce adulterous wives, but it was several decades before the same privilege was extended to wives with cheating husbands. Henry, of course, had Anne beheaded on the grounds that she cuckolded him. His next choice was the virginal Jane Seymour, who ended up dying from complications of giving birth to Henry's only male heir, Edward VI.

The Middle Ages, unlike our own time, placed a huge premium on virginity. (I say "unlike our own time" because I recently heard that about one in ten teens who pledge chastity keep that pledge until their wedding night.) Scholars now tend to believe that chastity belts were metaphor, not reality, in the Middle Ages. The common belief today is that actual chastity belts appeared in nineteenth-century England so women could protect themselves from unwanted advances by their employers in the workplace, and so parents could prevent children of both genders from masturbating.

You could say the medievals put the "Virgin" in the Virgin Mary, with their endless discussions of the virgin birth. Virgins also had the distinct advantage of being spared the risks of childbirth. There was a greater likelihood of independence for virgins as well. Sex, which was viewed more as a means to procreate than to recreate in the first place, was seen as a distraction from spirituality. Though Hildegard called Jesus her "sweetest hugger," and other virginal medieval mystics, including Catherine of Siena, believed they experienced marriage to Christ (Margery claimed Jesus told her to have a ring made inscribed with *Jesus est amor meus*, or "Jesus is my love"), there's no mention of sex in these unions. Even in more, um, conventional unions, medieval sex was viewed as less crucial to one's well-being than it is today. Both Marie d'Oignies and Margery experienced a surge of well-being and independence once their husbands agreed to chaste marriages. It isn't discussed much these days, but there's no shame in becoming a born-again virgin. In fact, it isn't unusual for widows to say that, over time, they discover their own bodies in ways unknown while they were married.

Can These Marriages Be Saved? Dorothea of Montau and Catherine of Genoa

Many of our mystics struggled with their marriages. Consider German mystic Dorothea of Montau (1347–1394), who maintained her spirituality despite horrendous pressure. She was married as a teenager to a swordsmith in his forties. As a newlywed, Dorothea began experiencing visions, which her husband was determined to beat out of her, complaining that she ignored her household duties: shopping, cooking, cleaning.

Given the lack of sanitation, household chores in medieval Europe were daunting—white sheets, for instance, were required to be clean enough to be able to see the fleas on them—a task generally reserved for women. In fact, bugs of all kinds were such a problem that some members of the wealthy classes hid a piece of animal fur on their person to discourage critters from burrowing in their own hair. Dorothea's household duties included caring for nine children, four of whom died in infancy and four of whom died during a round of the plague in 1383. (The surviving child, Gertrud, became a Benedictine nun.)

Perhaps Dorothea's husband had a change of heart, because eventually they made several pilgrimages together. While Dorothea was on a pilgrimage by herself to Rome, her husband died. After her return to what is now Germany, Dorothea became an anchoress, sought out because visitors found her many visions and revelations so helpful. Thank goodness, Dorothea's spirituality wasn't beaten out of her after all. Dorothea must have relied on her faith throughout her grief upon grief, and so her courage is helpful to remember when you need resolve to keep your faith. No doubt she found meaning in her painful experiences by counseling others.

Like Dorothea, Catherine of Genoa (1447–1510) also found herself in an abusive marriage, although the abuse was of the emotional and mental variety. Sweet, obedient Catherine Fieschi was married at fifteen to Guiliano Adorno, described as a man of "strange and recalcitrant nature," who fathered at least one child outside their marriage, though he and Catherine had no children of their own. By all accounts, the marriage was unhappy for over a decade, and apparently, Catherine spent the first five years in silent submission and the next five years trying to find happiness in the world.

By March 22, 1473, twenty-six-year-old Catherine was seriously depressed, and she paid a visit to one of her older sisters, Limbania, a nun at the convent to which Catherine had been denied entrance at age thirteen. Sister Limbania advised Catherine to make a confession. But while waiting for the priest, Catherine felt the presence of God so strongly that she was able to simultaneously bear the sense of her own sins and the deep love of God. "I live no longer," she proclaimed, "but Christ lives in me." Later, she reflected on the suddenness of her conversion, "Knowledge of God always comes in a rush."[8] She forgot all about confession and almost immediately began caring for the sick. She discovered a talent for administration and was named manager and treasurer of Pammatone Hospital for the poor of Genoa in 1490—no small feat for anyone, and especially remarkable for a medieval woman. Catherine's realm extended far beyond her desk out of necessity. Historians estimate that the plague outbreak of 1493 killed 80 percent of those who remained in the city. Although Catherine survived the outbreak, her work among the sick made her health precarious for the rest of her life.

Upon her conversion, Catherine must have surely wondered what to do about her disastrous marriage in a time when divorce wasn't an option. Her answer was to focus her sizeable energy on hospital work—she became a medieval, midlife, full-time working wife, while her husband continued to stray and spend extravagantly. Universally praised for her passion, Catherine fervently declared to God, "Even if I were in a camp of soldiers, I could not be prevented from loving you. If the world, or if the husband could impede love, what would such love be but a thing of weak and contemptible power?"[9] Over time, Catherine's love of God drew others, and so, ever the organizer, she formed several small groups of laypeople dedicated to prayer and serving the poor.

The meek and mild young Catherine had matured into a spunky, articulate woman.

It's not clear whether Catherine's husband's bankruptcy or his conversion came first, but they both happened around 1477, when Giuliano began helping Catherine care for Genoa's poor and ill. If he was at first disgusted by the conditions of the poor, Catherine was doubtlessly helpful, as she, a formerly sheltered aristocrat, had to overcome the same repugnance. Despite his profligate years, Giuliano dedicated the remainder of his life to ministry, caring for plague victims and the suffering of Genoa. Eventually, the Adornos lived in a simple home near the hospital, and Giuliano became a Franciscan tertiary, a layperson associated with the order. Over time, the couple recovered enough financially so they were able to work without pay. Giuliano died in 1497, leaving Catherine a widow for the remaining thirteen years of her life.

No contemporary woman can passively wait for an abusive husband to change as Giuliano did. But the story shows that there's always potential for growth in any human being, and therefore the potential for growth in human relationships. I wonder if Catherine learned this from Giuliano. Just as she understood that the compassion of nursing requires solid administration, Catherine's theology is passionately hopeful yet grounded in reality. She is known for her teaching that God's deep love for us brings us exquisite joy, while God's insistence on growing us in a sort of purification simultaneously brings us suffering.

Love and Loss, Then and Now: Widowhood and Divorce

Sometimes, in marriage as in life, suffering is described as a gift that makes growth possible. Some well-meaning person gave me a copy of *Necessary Losses* by Judith Viorst when I was new to widowhood, but I rejected the title so much that I refused to read the book. Perhaps my rejection had something to do with realizing that, whether I liked it or not, the author was on to something. Catherine described it in terms of the interplay between the joy of God's love and the suffering growth in God (and in ourselves), but both Catherine and Viorst accept that growth requires struggle.

In a section called "Healing through Pain" in *The Wisdom of Menopause: Creating Physical and Emotional Health and Healing During the Change*, physician Christiane Northrup observes, "Loss is a recurrent theme at midlife. Even women who don't go through divorce at this time often face other losses—the death of parents or spouse, estrangement from a child, being let go from a job, changes in physical appearance, or the realization that the reproductive years are over."[10]

One of the deep losses of midlife is sometimes divorce. According to the American Association of Retired Persons (AARP) study on divorce in midlife,[11] divorce over age fifty is on the rise, and the majority of midlife divorces (66 percent) are initiated by the wife. Why in midlife? About 58 percent of the men and 37 percent of the women polled say they postponed divorce until the children were raised.

The study underscores the painful circumstances that surround divorce. Respondents rated divorce as more devastating than losing a job, and almost as devastating as a spouse's death. Big issues, not a fleeting change of heart, seem to be root causes, particularly verbal, physical, or emotional abuse, with substance abuse not far behind. The greatest fear of divorce is the fear of being alone forever, and is, interestingly, most keenly felt among white people. Still, three out of four of the divorced people polled believe they made the right decision.

In the middle of divorce after two-dozen years of marriage that produced two daughters, Northrup found solace in a prayerful ritual. She writes,

> *I began a daily prayer practice to give me the courage to continue the process of letting go of my marriage and my identity as a married woman. This involved taking a walk every morning and stopping halfway through to look out over the harbor. There I would think about all that I had to be grateful for in my life—which was a lot. Then I would say a prayer of thanks out loud, sending the words down the river to its source.*[12]

Although Northrup's prayerful practice was born in the pain of divorce, it's probably worth a try anytime you're in so much pain that you need a reminder of all the things in your life for which you are grateful.

The thirteenth-century Persian poet Rumi looked to birds to learn about the difficulty and necessity of growth through pain:

The way of love is not
a subtle argument.
The door there
is devastation.
Birds make great sky-circles
of their freedom.
How do they learn it?
They fall, and falling,
they are given wings.[13]

Rumi's poem holds a special place in my heart because it accurately describes my experience as a widow. I never tell people it gets easier. I tell them that in my experience, although the pain doesn't lessen, you can grow stronger. You *can* live with the pain. Some days you'll fly further or more easily than others, but you *will* grow wings. Growing won't be easy, but the ways you grow can surprise you. I don't know if I would have become a priest if Scott had gotten well instead of dying from cancer, but I do know I would have been a different priest, a different mother, a different writer—a different everything. None of the differences are what I would have chosen, but I've come to learn that the differences in who I have become are valuable. I've had to learn to value different things about myself and about the world.

A year after Scott's death, Teddy, who had just turned three, and I left Pittsburgh. Scott and I had moved there six months after we married, settled into jobs we loved, made good friends, adopted a puppy, fixed up our starter house, and had our baby, the first, we hoped, of three—maybe four. It was a city we loved, full of people we loved, and, after Scott died, I heard myself saying over and over again that nothing fit anymore. I burst into tears every time I drove by a hospital where we'd been treated, avoided the sight of the animal shelter where we'd fallen in love with our mutt, saw memories of Scott holding Teddy's hand on every path of every park in Pittsburgh. I couldn't possibly avoid the pain enough to bear it. So we moved to New Haven, where I duked it out with God in divinity school while Teddy thrived in a wonderful preschool. We made friends. We grew. We survived. We learned that we could live without Scott, even if we didn't want to.

Elisabeth Kubler-Ross's observation that dying people and, by extension, grieving people, experience a variety of emotions—denial, anger, and so on—is useful. Grief's pattern is unpredictable, though, and the last thing dying or grieving people need to be told is that their grieving is somehow inadequate. Each person finds his or her own path through grief, whether it stems from divorce or death, and each path has opportunities to bring pain to God and to experience the healing that follows.

Many medieval widows found community in convents. Granted, several were forced by brothers or fathers into convents so they could get their hands on wealth (usually property) that rightly belonged to the women, but plenty of medieval women chose the religious life, including some widows who were probably relieved to be rid of abusive, unhappy, and otherwise exhausting marriages. Regardless of what their marriages had been like, living a life with other women that revolved around prayer offered widows both community and spiritual opportunities. Widows of means were more likely to choose to live in a convent, as it gave them security and independence from a father, brother, or new husband. These widows were usually boarders and, not infrequently, the men in charge of them were happy to pay for their keep so long as the men could retain their property. Often, the widows' numbers were so large they comprised a community within a community. Carrow outside Norwich, England, for example, housed up to 250 boarders, the majority of them widows, between the late fourteenth and mid-fifteenth centuries. Large numbers of widows are also known to have boarded in large numbers at La Murate in Florence.[14] Although few twenty-first-century widows (or divorcées) enter a convent, the fact that so many earlier unmarried middle-aged women have found solace in community is worth pondering.

According to Marla Paul, author of *The Friendship Crisis*, connection is increasingly important as the number of single American women continues to grow. In 2002, she reports, about 12 million American women were divorced, double the number of divorced women in this country in 1980. In 2002, 11 million widows lived in the United States, and that figure is predicted to increase as baby boomers age. The proportion of women in their early thirties who have never married has more than tripled in the past three decades, leaping from 6 percent to 22 percent. By 2010, it is projected that 31 million Americans will live alone.[15]

WELL LOVED: BIRGITTA OF SWEDEN

Our increasingly single world needs models like Brigitta of Sweden (c. 1303–1373). Like her fourteenth-century peer, Dorothea, Birgitta's piety deepened when she became single in midlife. Birgitta and her husband, Ulf, were the parents of eight children, among whom was St. Catherine of Sweden. Prior to her marriage—by all accounts a happy one, though she was a thirteen-year-old bride and he was an eighteen-year-old groom—Birgitta had experienced a deep sense of God's love, and even some visions. It wasn't until age forty-one, when the responsibilities of family life were diminished by Ulf's death and children leaving home, that Birgitta's spiritual life reopened, this time on an even deeper level. Birgitta was visited regularly by both Jesus and the Virgin Mary, who assured her that she was as well loved as a virgin as she had been as a wife as she was as a widow.

Wealthy and noble through both birth and marriage, Birgitta was able to hang onto her money and property upon Ulf's death and found a monastery. Over time, Birgitta became convinced that her visions were worth sharing, and when word got out, she became something of a celebrity. Still, it took her twenty years from the time she arrived in Rome to be granted an audience by Pope Urban V, who granted her permission to form a new order, though he turned a deaf ear to her criticism of the church in general. Nevertheless, in 1999, Pope John Paul II named Birgitta the patron saint of Europe.

When Birgitta died at age seventy, she was well known for her charity, her spiritual visions, and her leadership. Perhaps most significantly for us, she had demonstrated that women who become single again have much to contribute to the world.

———————

Regardless of your marital status, there is always God. Virgins have examples of women of faith by the score. Remember Hildegard calling Jesus "her sweetest hugger"? Married women have models such as Catherine of Genoa. Divorced women, who sometimes say they get along better with their former husband after a divorce than before, may find echoes of their own stories in those of Marie and Margery. Widowed women can look to Dorothea and Birgitta. Whether you're lonely or happily married or in the middle of divorcing, Catherine of Genoa's words can help: "In this world, the rays of God's love, unbeknownst to us, encircle us all about."

A Prayer to Get Started

God who is faithful to all people, married, divorced, partnered, single, thank you for loving us no matter who else does or doesn't. Thank you for all the chances you give us to grow in this world. Thank you for revealing yourself throughout the changes of our lives.

Thank you for receiving all our emotions, no matter how conflicted or confusing or ugly. Teach us to welcome healing even as we hate the reasons we need it. Draw us closer to you as we struggle in our human relationships. Help us understand that ultimately we belong to you, and not to one another. In the name of you, whom Catherine of Genoa taught us can always transform our souls, Amen.

QUESTIONS FOR JOURNALING AND REFLECTION

1. What has your life taught you about marriage? Staying single? Being widowed? Getting divorced? Write a letter to a younger woman sharing your wisdom. What does your wisdom say about your experience of God in your life?

2. Catherine of Genoa has a lot to say about difficult times bringing us closer to God. What do you think? In terms of your life, is Catherine on to something? Has your suffering affected your spirituality? How?

3. There are lots of statistics in this chapter. Which surprised you the most? Which did you know were true all along? Which popped out for you? Why do you think that is?

4. Catherine wrote about the fiery love of God:

    These rays purify and then annihilate.
    The soul becomes like gold
    that becomes purer as it is fired,
    all dross being cast out.

    Having come to the point of twenty-four carats,
    gold cannot be purified any further;
    and this is what happens to the soul
    in the fire of God's love.[16]

5. How would you describe the love of God? Is it like rays? Like a hug? Like a distant mountain? What in your life has purified you? How? And what have you become?

9

MOTHERING WITHOUT SMOTHERING

Next time you're reminded how difficult motherhood is, think of Dhuoda of Septimania, who found a way to love her children even though she wasn't allowed near them. We don't know a lot about Dhuoda (c. 806/11–after 843), but we know enough to understand that she left a legacy of love. Born into nobility, she somehow picked up Latin along the way. We don't know where Dhuoda's from, but we know that in 824, she married Bernard, duke of Septimania, located in what is now southeastern France, and had two sons, William and Bernard junior, born fifteen years apart. In between these births, the duke fell out of favor. As proof that he supported Charles the Bald, a.k.a. Charles II of France and the Holy Roman Empire, Bernard sent William at age fifteen to serve at court. Dhuoda knew she'd never see William again. What's more, she had just given birth to Bernard junior and, before he had even been baptized, the baby was whisked away to his father in Aquitaine. Dhuoda knew she had lost both her children for good.

As a way to continue loving her children, Dhuoda wrote

A Handbook for My Warrior Son William, which she hoped William would follow and share with his younger brother. You get a sense of how desperately Dhuoda wanted to communicate with her children, as she used all manner of devices to get their attention: word games, number games, biblical stories told in a simple style, examples from literature and from everyday life. "My son," she wrote,

> *you will have learned doctors to teach you many more examples, more eminent and of greater usefulness, but they are not of equal status with me, nor do they have a heart more ardent than I, your mother, have for you, my firstborn son . . . and when your little brother, whose name I do not even know as yet, has received the grace of baptism in Christ, do not be slow to teach, encourage and love him, to rouse him to go from good to better. When he shall have reached the age of speaking and reading, show him this little volume, this Handbook which I have written and composed in your name.*[1]

Dhuoda's "little volume" consisted of over seventy-three chapters conveying the mother's love and solid advice. Love God first, she advised. Be patient. Timing is everything. "When metal-smiths endeavor to work gold to the proper thinness for applying gilt leaf, they wait for a desirable and propitious day, time, hour and temperature so that this bright, shimmering, precious metal will take on an even more striking brilliance and will be more malleable for decorative use."[2]

Sadly, Dhuoda's husband was executed for treason around the time she died, and William was killed in battle trying to avenge his father's lands. We know Bernard junior lived long enough to father two children, but it's a toss-up whether he died peacefully or at the hands of an executioner.

In many ways, Dhuoda exemplifies what it means to be a good mother, even when your children no longer live in your home. It just means to keep on praying for them. To keep on loving, even when it's hard—especially when it's hard. It's not easy to remember how important it is to mother to a child's developmental stage, but Julian of Norwich's theology contains advice from the time children are in diapers through independence. She also understood that the child inside each of us never disappears. She mused,

A mother may allow her child sometimes to fall, and to learn the hard way, for its own good. But because she loves the child she will never allow the situation to become dangerous. Admittedly earthly mothers have been known to let their children die, but our heavenly Mother, Jesus, will never let us, his children die. He and none but he is almighty, all wisdom, all love. Blessings on him! But often when we are shown the extent of our fall and wretchedness we are so scared and dreadfully ashamed that we scarcely know where to look. But our patient Mother does not want us to run away: nothing would be more displeasing to him. His desire is that we should do what a child does: for when a child is in trouble or scared it runs to its mother for help as fast as it can. Which is what he wants us to do, saying with the humility of a child, "Kind, thoughtful, dearest Mother, do be sorry for me. I have got myself into a filthy mess, and am not a bit like you. I cannot begin to put it right without your special and willing help." Even if we do not feel immediate relief we can still be sure that he behaves like a wise mother. If he sees it is better for us to mourn and weep he lets us do so—with pity and sympathy, of course, and for the right length of time—because he loves us.

*And he wants us to copy the child who always and
naturally trusts mother's love through thick and thin.*[3]

Julian's intimate knowledge of mothering and children
naturally makes us wonder if she was a mother herself. Many
have conjectured that Julian understood suffering so well because
she had lost children (or other loved ones) to the plague. The
whole issue of Julian's motherhood—or not—is complicated,
because medievals were not as child-centered as we are in the
twenty-first century. Consider this: Julian's visitor, Margery of
Kempe, mentions only one of her fourteen children, a son who
died in adulthood, in her autobiography. The context is that
Margery and her foreign daughter-in-law, who eventually
returned to what is now Germany with her child, didn't get along
well after the son died. Perhaps it was misplaced grief, a conflict
of temperament, linguistic, and cultural gaps; in any case, it isn't
difficult to imagine Margery as a formidable mother-in-law.

Still, Julian's insight that good mothering tailors care to the
child's developmental age is lasting. In fact, her medieval insight is
buttressed by work at the Adolescent Study Center at Columbia
University. Researchers conclude that when girls are treated as if
they're older than they actually are, their risk for depression is
increased throughout their lives. Also among their findings,
reassuringly, is that mothers and daughters form a most intense
emotional pair, and that the relationship is most charged during
adolescence[4]—which goes a long way toward explaining the
amount of fighting between most mothers and teenage daughters.

MOTHER-DAUGHTER BONDS: CATHERINE OF SIENA
Lapa Piagenti Benincasa, Catherine of Siena's mother, probably
knew all about the intensity of mothering teenage daughters. In
the first place, Catherine was the twenty-third of twenty-five
children. (The twenty-fourth child, her twin sister, died at birth.)

In the second place, if Lapa didn't learn how challenging it can be to be a mother from the first twenty-two children, I'm sure Catherine taught her. Saint Catherine may have led countless followers to the edges of heaven, but as a teenager, she drove her mother to distraction.

In 1347, Catherine Benincasa (1347–1380) was born in the district of Siena, Italy, to a cloth dyer and his wife, Lapa. Perhaps the size of her family had something to do with Catherine's reported vow of virginity at age seven. She refused to do as her mother wished and become a wife, and she also refused to be a nun. Instead, the old maid became a Dominican tertiary at age sixteen: she took less strict vows and continued living in her home, though she dressed in the black and white habit of a Dominican nun. Like Frank Sinatra, Catherine insisted on doing it her way.

For three years, Catherine left her room only for Mass and confession, ate only herbs, and slept only a few hours each night. And you thought *your* teenager had strange habits! Something had to give, and Catherine was persuaded to join the world again, to help around the house and to leave the house to care for the poor and the ill. Over time, the downtrodden of Siena called Catherine "Our Holy Mother." By then, she had come to the conclusion that "there is no perfect virtue—one that bears fruit—unless it is exercised by means of our neighbor."[5] In other words, it's what you do with your prayer, what you do for others in this world, that really matters. The story of Catherine's turn from navel gazer to selfless giver is useful to remember when you wonder if your grown child will ever grow beyond him- or herself.

Catherine went way beyond herself, becoming an integral player in late fourteenth-century politics. It all started because she was a gifted listener. As her reputation spread, the lowly and the high of Siena society streamed to her for spiritual direction and for her insight into reconciliation, especially when it came to settling old family feuds. The church had a feud of its own brewing between those who were happy to have the pope in Avignon and those who believed the church had grown corrupt in its relocation to the south of France. Several republics in what is now northern Italy had declared war against the pope, though historians quickly point out that the Florentines and their cohorts were less interested in reforming the church than in furthering their own political gains.

If you've ever visited the imposing papal palace in Avignon, France, you can imagine how intimidating it must have felt to Catherine as she stood in its formidable shadows. Built on an enormous natural rock that overlooks the town, the building is a first-rate fortress, with walls over seventeen feet thick. Between 1309 and 1377, seven popes ruled there, indulging in various degrees of corruption, vanity, and loose living. But as war was brewing in her native Tuscany, Catherine gathered her courage, made the arduous journey to Avignon, and met with Pope Gregory XI. She recommended that, first, he return the papacy to Rome, turning his back on the life of ease he and top administrators enjoyed in Provence; second, that he reform the clergy, including himself; and third, that he launch a crusade to claim the land of Jesus for Christians, and perhaps to win converts from Islam.

In the end, Gregory returned the papacy to Rome (though schisms continued—and Catherine was compelled to write to a hot-headed successor, Pope Urban VI, "For the love of Christ crucified, restrain a little those hasty movements of your nature!"). Clerical reform happened after Catherine died, but with the aid of some of her followers. And there was no crusade. In the meantime, Catherine spent a good deal of her short life as a sort of fourteenth-century Condoleezza Rice, patching up micro-feuds between Siena's Hatfields and McCoys and macro-feuds between Pisa and Florence. By 1376, so many gathered to hear Catherine wherever she traveled that a papal bull was issued requiring that three priests accompany her to hear the confessions of her fans.

A story that reveals the steely backbone of this reconciler, no doubt shaped in the sullen teenager's room, goes like this. When Catherine went to Avignon to speak with the pope, she wasn't welcome or trusted. As she knelt in prayer, a lady-in-waiting stuck a long needle in her foot, but Catherine was too focused on prayer to notice.

By this time, Catherine and her mother were on slightly easier terms. With love on both sides, Catherine still insisted on independence. Read closely, and you'll also hear a longing for acceptance. From Avignon, Catherine wrote Lapa:

Dearest Mother,

How I have longed to see you truly the mother of my soul as well as of my body! . . . You know that I must follow God's will, and I know that you want me to follow it. It was God's will that I go away—and my going was not without mystery, nor without worthwhile results. It was also God's will that I remain away; it was no mere human decision. . . . You were glad, I remember, for the sake of material gain when your sons left home to win temporal wealth. But now when it is a question of winning eternal life it seems to be so hard that you say you are going to go to pieces if I don't answer you soon. All this because you love the part of me that I got from you (I mean your flesh, in which you clothed me) more than you love the part of me that I got from God. Lift, lift up your heart and affection a bit to that dear most holy cross, where every burden becomes light.[6]

EMPTY NESTS

With relationships with our children so complex, it's to be expected that their leaving the nest leaves us with a mixture of emotions. Although popular myth depicts women whose children are launched as depressed and at loose ends, there's more to the story than grief. According to a 2002 study by the National Association of Social Workers, "Women at Midlife: Life Experiences and Implications for the Helping Professions," children's leaving home isn't necessarily devastating. Nobody's suggesting you won't experience a stew of emotions when your kids have flown the nest but, according to the study, "More often than not, the positives of this period of life outweigh the negatives." In fact, many fifty-something women feel a deep satisfaction in raising and launching children—alongside excitement at having the time to explore their own talents and abilities.[7]

The study didn't examine spirituality but, if it had, I bet it would conclude that many women find there's room for deepened spirituality in the empty nest. Middle age raises many questions about mortality and how you're going to spend the rest of your life. In addition, many of us have more unstructured time as we age, so it's no wonder middle age is often a time for spiritual exploration.

MARY: THE MOTHER OF MEDIEVAL MOTHERS

The longing for the feminine side of God, for a divine understanding of a woman's experience, seems to be timeless. It was a long time coming. In 431, at the Council of Ephesus, theologians determined that Mary was "Theotokos," Greek for "God-bearer." She came to be seen as a compassionate mediator between suffering mankind and her son, Jesus, who was seen as King and Judge. After all, at the wedding in Cana, Mary persuaded Jesus to perform his first miracle of turning water into wine (John 2:1–12). Early Christian art shows both Mary and the baby Jesus wearing crowns.

By the twelfth century, the cult of the Virgin Mary was in place, inspiring the Ave Maria prayer[8] and countless works of art—stained glass, plays, poems, sculptures, paintings—dedicated to her. Right through the Rennaissance, painters usually portrayed Mary in ultramarine blue, the costliest pigment. Bernard of Clairvaux (1090–1153) identified Mary as the beautiful bride in the Song of Solomon. Especially in France, cathedrals were named for her. Chartres cathedral, arguably the most magnificent of these architectural homages, was built in the late twelfth and early thirteenth centuries and contains what was purported to be her veil. It has been called "a toy-house to please the Queen of Heaven—to please her so much that she would be happy in it,—to charm her till she smiled."[9]

Historian Thomas Cahill writes,

> *Mary, formerly peasant girl of Nazareth, now Queen of Heaven, was given so much publicity that she came to overshadow her divine son in popular devotion and ecclesiastical art. It is not so surprising that . . . [Mary's] cult, whether of flesh and blood or of stone and stained glass, should be especially vibrant in Germanic and Celtic realms [including modern France and the British Isles], where women in pagan times held more power than they ever exercised in the Greco-Roman world.[10]*

Cahill's nineteenth-century predecessor Henry Adams credited the Virgin with a kind of creative energy that permeated medieval art, calling her, "the highest energy ever known to man, the creator of four-fifths of his noblest art, exercising vastly more attraction over the human mind than all the steam-engines and dynamos ever dreamed of. . . . All the steam in the world could not, like the Virgin, build Chartres."[11] Notre Dame of Chartres, and indeed all those medieval French cathedrals—Notre Dame of Paris, Notre Dame of Rheims, and so on—reflect that Mary had become "Our Lady." As such, she was an inspirational counterpart to the ladies of courtly love, the lifestyle that sparked so much adultery. Mary was firmly in place as the New Eve, a redeemer, especially for women, providing hope that if you were suffering from the plague or feared child-birth, a gentle, caring, sinless woman would pray for you.

Birgitta of Sweden, who claims that of her eight children, only one named Karl—always in trouble as a youngster, in bed with married women as an adult—caused her any worry. Birgitta came to understand that she was to love God even more than her children, and that a mother's prayer is powerful. After Karl's death of tuberculous in 1372, Brigitta was comforted by Mary, who served as a kind of midwife to his soul. The Virgin had stood by Karl's deathbed, "as a womman that standith by another womman when sche childeth, to help the chylde that it dye not of flowying of bloode ne be no slayne in the streight place were it cometh oute."[12]

While medievals understood Mary as worthy of veneration and able to profoundly affect our world, they also saw her as an intimate. Since 1223, when Francis of Assisi assembled the first crèche, Mary has been depicted every Christmas as a very human mother, suckling her babe. As the Stations of the Cross developed among those who found it increasingly difficult to make the pilgrimage to Jerusalem, Mary's role as grieving mother was emphasized as well.

This medieval view of Mary as both Queen of Heaven and earthly mother, virgin *and* God-bearer, otherwordly *and* accessible, is empowering for us twenty-first-century types. Mary shows us that we can be both powerful and loving, that we can survive swords piercing our souls (Luke 2:25), that no matter how humble our origins, no matter how checkered our past (Mary was an unwed teenage mother, remember), we can grow into the women God created us to be. No matter who we are, there are many parts of us, and God loves them all.

Perhaps because medievals, in their fascination with Jesus' humanity, had discovered Jesus' mother, some of them discovered the motherliness of Jesus as well, and that point of view speaks to many of us today.

AND MORE MEDIEVAL MOTHER FIGURES

Noticing Bible passages such as Jesus' lament to gather Jerusalem's children as a hen gathers her brood under her wings (Matthew 23:37; Luke 13:34), a few Christians from at least the fourth century have compared Jesus to a mother. Even the venerable saints Anselm of Canterbury (c. 1033–1109) and Bernard of Clairvaux recognized Jesus as a divine mother. But perhaps no one has done more for Jesus' motherhood than Julian, who saw Jesus as the epitome of motherhood (she also saw Jesus as the epitome of fatherhood, and as the best medieval lord). She likened Jesus' passion on the cross to childbirth, his sharing the Eucharist to a mother's sharing of breast milk, his care to a mother's loving discipline. She put it this way:

> *A mother's [love] is the most intimate, willing and dependable of all services, because it is the truest of all. None has been able to fulfill it properly but Christ, and he alone can. We know that our own mother's bearing of us was a bearing to pain and death, but what does Jesus, our true mother do? Why, he, All-love, bears us to joy and eternal life!*[13]

If Julian had lost children to the plague, or even to distance, it's easy to understand the comfort she found in understanding

Jesus as the perfect mother. Not only does Jesus give us new life, his love for us is so profound that he never leaves us, even becoming one of us. "So Jesus is our true Mother in nature by our first creation, and He is our true Mother in grace by His taking our created nature."

Teresa of Avila had a slightly different outlook, likening our souls to nursing infants at the breast of Christ. She wrote,

> *The soul is like an infant that still nurses at it mother's breast, and the mother without her babe's effort to suckle puts the milk in its mouth in order to give it delight. So it is here; for without effort of the intellect the will is loving, and the Lord desires that the will, without thinking about the matter, understand that it is with Him and that it does no more than swallow the milk His Majesty places in its mouth, and enjoy that sweetness.*[14]

Marguerite d'Oingt (d. 1310) is another medieval Christian who found motherhood in Jesus. She wrote poetically in both Latin and Franco-Provençal, the language of her people. The prioress of a Carthusian house, Marguerite blamed a chronic illness on her visions, and found the cure by writing them down to share with others. She wrote about herself in third person:

> *[Her visions] . . . were all written in her heart in such a way that she could not think about anything else. . . . She thought that if she were to put these things in writing, as Our Lord had sent them to her in her heart, her heart would be more relived for it. She began to write everything that is in this book. . . . as soon as she put a word in the book, it left her heart. . . . I firmly believe that if she had not put it in writing she would have died or become crazy.*[15]

In addition to leaving us her cautionary tale on the importance of expressing yourself, Marguerite left us her image of Jesus as mother. She prayed:

> *Are you not my mother and more than my mother? The mother who bore me labored in delivering me for one day or one night, but you, my sweet and lovely Lord, labored for me for more than thirty years. Ah, . . . with what love you labored for me and bore me through your whole life. But when the time approached for you to be delivered, your labor pains were so great that your body sweat was like great drops of blood that came out from your body and fell on the earth. . . . when the hour of your delivery came you were placed on the hard bed of the cross . . . and your nerves and all your veins were broken. And truly it is no surprise that your veins burst when in one day you gave birth to the whole world.*[16]

MEDIEVAL MOTHERING

It would be interesting to know how including motherhood in their image of the divine influenced our mystics in their mothering, but there's no evidence to tell us. Not all our mystics were mothers, but Hadewijch of Brabant (the area around Antwerp), who lived in the early 1200s, is a good example of a woman who recognized the relationship of God and motherhood in others. Hadewijch had a knack for passing on good and loving advice to younger women. One such woman, Sara, struggled mightily with receiving visions (perhaps not unlike Hildegard and Marguerite d'Oingt). Eventually, Hadewijch reported, Sara "came back to herself, and having received 74 lovely revelations and also the spirit of prophecy; she also had true works of charity—something that surpasses all the rest. She had the Holy

Spirit in her soul and in her body. With all her exercises [of virtue], she was a perfect mother of God."[17]

This idea of a human being's behavior giving birth to God is radical at first glance (as is the idea of Jesus as our mother), but so is the depth of God's deep yearning for our love and for our help in the world, as I was reminded by a recent Christmas card. In deep blue calligraphy, the card proclaimed, "We are meant to be mothers of God for God is always needing to be born." That insight is from Meister Eckhart von Hochheim (1260–1328), a Dominican from what is now Germany. He was addressed as "Meister" or "Master" in honor of his status as a learned professor of theology in Paris and elsewhere. Nevertheless, when Meister Eckhart died, he was in the middle of a heresy trial. Obviously a learned man, he also had a mystical side like Teresa, reminding us that God needs us.

MOTHERHOOD, THEN AND NOW

Whether we are mothers or not, and, if we are, no matter what kind of mothers we or our offspring think we were or are, we're what God has on this earth, and so God needs our help. This is not because God is weak; it is because God's love for us is so strong.

As I write this, my only child is finishing his junior year in boarding school. Possibly the most important thing Ted learned this year was from his chemistry teacher. The lesson I'm referring to has nothing to do with scientific knowledge; I'm referring to his having to learn to cope with a difficult authority figure. Surely, facing that challenge with a teacher will help prepare him for difficult bosses in the future. My challenge these days is learning to step back; otherwise, Ted's not going to realize that he can cope with challenges like difficult people. And, healthy adolescent that he is, Ted will react by pushing me away if he senses that I'm paving the way for him.

Yet, I still need to communicate with my maturing son. Dhuoda inspires me to send him newspaper clippings I think would interest him. Sometimes, I even sneak in an article about the perils of smoking or drunk driving. Julian reminds me that sometimes being a good mother means refraining from rescuing children, allowing offspring to make mistakes so they can learn from them. And, of course, I take heart that even when Ted is at his most adolescent, I still have an easier time than Catherine of Siena's mother did!

A DAUGHTER ALL YOUR LIFE

One of the gifts of being a mother is the opportunity to come to terms with our own mother. For some of us, this is easier than for others. If your daughterhood is marked with the knowledge that you confused or otherwise let your parents down, you have the company of Clare of Assisi, who disappointed her parents, Ortolana and Monaldo Offreduccio. Disappointment was not what Claire's parents expected (whom among us does?). When Ortolana knelt in one of Assisi's churches to pray for a safe delivery, she heard a voice emanating from the crucifix: "Fear not, woman, for you shall bring forth without danger a light that shall greatly illumine the world." When the baby came, on July 16, 1194, she was given the name Chiara, meaning "bright" or "light" in Italian. Nevertheless, this eldest daughter brought her share of storms to the family.

As Clare was growing up, Francis of the same town was giving his family a run for their money. While literally rebuilding San Damiano, a small dilapidated church outside Assisi, Francis suddenly blurted out, "Here there will be an order of ladies whose fame and holy life will glorify the heavenly Father in his whole church." Francesco must have been shocked, because he, an Italian, was speaking French. Francis and his followers, who were growing in number, understandably kept the outburst quiet, but more and more of Assisi's citizens heard him preach over time. Clare was among these folks, and she determined to lead a life more similar to the one Francis was leading than than the one her parents desired for her, which involved finding a nice boy and settling down to a life like theirs. The Palm Sunday when Clare was fifteen, she left her family home via the *porta del morto* or "door of the dead," used solely for the purpose of bearing the dead from the house. Although she was very much alive, Clare intended to never re-enter the house, and so far as we know, she never did.

Clare's family and fiancé were outraged. By the time her male relatives found her, she had taken haven in the Church of San Paolo, and as they tried to pry Clare from the altar, her hood fell down, revealing her shorn head. Francis had agreed to cut her hair in another symbol that she was leaving her worldly life behind. Shocked, the men retreated, and Francis's followers took her to a convent, San Angela di Panzo, in the hills overlooking Assisi. The story might have ended there, but Clare's younger sister, Agnes, followed her sister, riling up the family all over again. When they found out where the sisters were hiding, a dozen male relatives were again dispatched, and they actually laid their hands on Agnes, but were unable to move her because she'd grown so heavy, they complained, "It's as if she'd been eating lead."[18] A further detail to the story is that Monaldo, beside himself with rage, drew his sword to strike one of his daughters, but his arm dropped, withered and useless, by his side.

Over time, Clare and Agnes made an uneasy peace with their family of origin. Together, they founded the order that is known today as the Poor Clares, emphasizing Clare's insistence—even to the Pope—that the things of this life impair our spiritual growth. Clare's life is intertwined with Francis's, and history agrees that they strengthened one another's ministry. Yet at best,

Clare seems to have remained a puzzle to her family. Years ago, I saw a cartoon of a statue. It was of a man on a mighty steed and the plaque on him commemorated him as "Soldier, Statesman, Poet—And Still a Disappointment to His Mother." I have a feeling Clare could commiserate.

It's too bad Clare, the thirteenth century Italian, didn't know Julian, the fourteenth century Englishwoman, because the anchoress offers some comfort. By reminding us that we are born of God, and that Jesus is, at least in some sense, our perfect mother, Julian claims that the divine loves us in the style of American children's television neighbor, Mister Rogers, just the way we are. None of us have (or are) perfect mothers. But we all have the need for one.

When Julian stressed that we are enclosed in God, she reminded us that we are daughters of God. "For just as the body is clothed in its garments, and the flesh in its skin, and the bones in their flesh, and the heart in its body, so too are we, soul and body, clothed from head to foot in the goodness of God. Yes, and even more closely than that, for all these things will decay and wear out, whereas the goodness of God is unchanging, and incomparably more suited to us."[19] Julian suggested that God holds us within in much the way a woman carries a child in her womb. She said of Jesus, "Indeed, our Savior himself is our Mother for we are for ever being born of him, and shall never be delivered!"[20] This idea of being a beloved daughter of the divine can bring enormous comfort if you feel you fell short of your parents' hopes or if they fell short of yours.

Perhaps the relationship between Catherine of Siena and her mother was complicated by the timeless dynamic of mothers offering advice their daughters feel as criticism.[21] In any case, there seems to be a theme of Catherine defending herself that runs through her letters home, and for whatever reasons, Catherine seeks to assure her widowed mother of her love.

While on a mission to reconcile warring clans, she writes, "Understand, dearest mother, that I your poor daughter have been put on earth for no other purpose; this is what my Creator has chosen me for. I know that you are happy to have me obey him. If you think I am staying here longer than you would like, I beg you to be content, because I cannot do otherwise. I believe that if you knew the circumstances you yourself would be sending me here."[22]

Who among us can't identify with Catherine's desire to be both a beloved daughter and herself? Navigating that struggle continues well beyond leaving home, or even our mother's death. My own mother lives in a haze of late-stage Alzheimer's. The water lily in this heartbreaking swamp is that she receives good care in the advanced Alzheimer's unit of a nursing home in my home town, half-way across the country. She hasn't known anyone for a few years, and at this point rarely makes sounds of any kind, let alone words. Visiting Mom is more for myself than for her, and mostly consists of my stroking her hand and my doing all the talking. The best way I have to visit with her these days is to read from the psalms. On my last visit, I came in the evening and she'd already been put to bed. Through misty eyes, I leafed through my Book of Common Prayer and found lines that spoke of hope and peace and eternity, and the psalms and I read her to sleep.

Hadewijch of Brabant once wrote a letter to a younger member of her community under distressing circumstances. It sounds to me as if it could be written by a mother with Alzheimer's, or who has suffered a dehabilitating stroke, or who already passed:

"Think about it yourself; if you believe with all your heart that I am loved by God, and he is doing his work in me, secretly or openly, and that he renews his old wonders in me, you must also be aware that these are doings of Love..."[23]

Hadewijch's phrase, "the doings of Love," applies better than anything else I've ever heard to what we try to do as loving mothers and caring daughters, no matter what our circumstances.

A PRAYER TO GET STARTED

God who brings us to life, and who labors all our lives long to help us know you cherish us, thank you for your complexity. Thank you for always having more to reveal to us, even when our nests are empty. Thank you for the rich variety of people—including children—who teach us about you. Open our hearts and minds and wills to all you have to teach us about yourself. Open us to the ways of loving each other that your being reflects. Open us to medieval mothers and all they have to teach us about you. Grow us into inquisitive and open souls that reflect your love. In the name of you, whom Teresa taught needs us, Amen.

QUESTIONS FOR JOURNALING AND REFLECTION

1. Have you ever connected motherhood and the divine? How does it feel to think of Jesus as a mother? How does including the image of the divine as mother impact your spirituality? If you're a mother, how does including the image of the divine as mother impact your mothering?

2. If, like Dhuoda, you knew you would never see your children (or others you mother) again, what advice would you write for them? In what ways is it similar or different from advice your own mother gave you?

3. Catherine of Siena insisted on doing things her way, refusing to marry or become a nun, for instance, and telling off popes. She seems to have been completely herself, and perhaps this was part of the fruit of her prayer. Have you ever noticed, in yourself or in others, prayer bringing the self to the forefront?

4. Beatrice wrote that "Love makes the soul so bold that it no longer fears man nor friend, angel or saint or God Himself."[24] At what points in your life has this statement rung the most, or the least, true?

10

OFFICE POLITICS

When I was in my mid-twenties and fishing for a career, the "placement lady"—which was what everybody called her—in the renowned school of journalism where I was completing an M.A. advised me to marry my boyfriend and follow him. "He's getting an MBA, right? So he'll always make more money." I was vaguely upset, but wasn't yet evolved enough to articulate the reasons. Left to my own devices, I landed a job in an accounting firm's public relations office, where I learned the meaning of the old saw about square pegs and round holes. I wanted the job because I was attracted to prestige and corner offices. But I knew I was miserable, so I kept trying to figure out what I was doing wrong (the only strategy I knew back then was to blame myself). Along the way, I picked up a book that advised me to study sports and war, as these were the only things men, who ran the world, understood. It also advised that if a man ever asked me to get him a cup of coffee, I should "accidentally" spill it on his crotch. Though it was years before I realized how demeaning the book was to both genders, I never actually scalded anyone. These were the days when women wore bows—pseudo-ties—around our necks and suits with padded shoulders, showing the boys we could at least dress like them. We didn't quite know what else to do but be women in men's clothing.

One of the most enduring things I recall reading on the subject of how to be a working woman in a man's world was a poster about geese, who rotate leadership of the flock during migration. Dhuoda of Septimania used stags as an example of leadership, reminding her sons:

> *Stags habitually behave in the following way: When a stag sets out to swim across bodies of water, or wide rivers with turbulent currents, one stag after the other lays its head and horns on the back of the one before it. By resting a little, they may quickly and more easily cross the water. They are so intelligent and have such subtle instinct that when they sense the leader is beginning to flag, they let him drop back to second place and choose the rearmost stag to swim at the head, so as to support and refresh the others. This way, as each changes places with all the others in turn, a fraternal creaturely kindness surges through all of them.*[1]

I wonder if Dhuoda would have found kindness surging through the concept of mentoring, enjoying renewed popularity more than eleven hundred years after her death. I sometimes think it was the healthiest impulse we had back in the 1980s, when "mentoring" seemed to flow off every tongue at every networking event. Though the story of Mentor assisting in the education and training of young Telemachus in Homer's epics may have been familiar to some educated people in the Middle Ages, the concept of mentoring—encouragement with empathy—definitely was not. Nevertheless, anchoresses provide a model of mentoring. Of the young women who made sure Julian of Norwich received enough to eat and otherwise cared for her needs while she was an anchoress, at least one of them, Alice, became an anchoress herself. Outside the anchorage, two sets of mentor-mentored—Clare of Assisi and Agnes of Prague from the thirteenth century, Hildegard of Bingen and Elisabeth of Schonau from the twelfth century—model healthy relationships through their letters.

MENTORING WOMEN, MEDIEVAL STYLE

Clare mentored all her followers, and by the end of her life, over a hundred communities were based on her teaching. She wanted townspeople to look at the community of Poor Clares and see the love of Christ in action, and advised her nuns to take Jesus Christ as their "mirror," or, as we might say, "mentor." Clare wrote her nuns,

> *For the Lord Himself has placed us not only as a form for others in being an example and mirror, but even for our sisters whom the Lord has called to our way of life as well, that they in turn might be a mirror and example to those living in the world. Since the Lord has called us to such great things that those who are to be a mirror and example to others may be reflected in us, we are greatly bound to bless and praise God and be all the more strengthened to do good in the Lord.[2]*

A century later, Angela of Foligno was inspired by Clare's ideas of mirroring Christ to the world in her calling as a lay woman serving the poor of greater Assisi (Foligno was a suburb of Assisi). Perhaps Angela was mentored by Clare to believe in her visions enough to write for her *own* followers—toward whom, remember, she felt herself a sort of mother.

Hildegard of Bingen shared the idea of mirroring with Elisabeth of Schonau. The importance of Hildegard's place in Elisabeth's life comes into focus when you realize that other than the journey from her hometown of Bonn to Schonau, where she joined the mixed monastery of men and women at age twelve, the only other trip she undertook was to visit Hildegard. It seems Elisabeth was finding receiving visions burdensome, and she knew that fellow seer Hildegard could help. In fact, it was a vision that prompted her to make the pilgrimage.

Long after the visit, Hildegard encouraged Elisabeth through letters. "O my daughter," she wrote, "may God make you a mirror of life. I too cower in the puniness of my mind, and am greatly wearied by anxiety and fear. Yet from time to time I resound a little, like a dim sound of a trumpet from the Living Light."[3] While recognizing the difficulties of bearing such a deep sensitivity, Hildegard buoyed Elisabeth by desiring for her that her soul reflect God.

No matter what your life situation, thinking of yourself as a mirror can go a long way toward your becoming the kind of mentor you want to be for the younger women (and men) in your life. Ask yourself if you're behaving in a way you'd like younger women to pass on to your granddaughters. And if you're frustrated by not being able to put the kind of time into mentoring that you wish you could, you're in good company. Clare of Assisi felt the same way in her relationship to Agnes.

Agnes, princess of Bohemia, is proof that being a princess isn't all it's cracked up to be—perhaps in much the same way that getting a corner office isn't everything today. Sent north as a baby to be married to a duke of part of what is now Poland, she was returned to Prague at age three when her fiancé died. Shortly thereafter, Agnes was promised to a son of Emperor Frederick II and sent to Austria—where she was rejected, and sent home again. Agnes's father planned to go to war over the jilting, but apparently, Agnes, gentle as a lamb (which is what "Agnes" means in Latin), talked him out of it. Besides, he was busy entertaining marriage proposals for Agnes from suitors in England and from the Emperor Frederick himself. In the meantime, Agnes had heard about Clare of Assisi and felt called to live a similar life. In a surprisingly generous move for his time, Agnes's father agreed and even financed a convent where Agnes was a member.

Unlike Hildegard and Elisabeth, Clare and Agnes never met. Their relationship evolved exclusively through letters, with Clare taking on the role of mentor to Agnes. Shortly before her death, Clare penned, "If I have not written to you as often as your soul—and mine as well—desire and long for, do not wonder, or think that the fire of love for you glows with less delight in the heart of your mother. No, this is the difficulty: the lack of messengers and the obvious dangers of the roads."[4]

My guess is that though she would have appreciated more letters, Agnes found what Clare was able to send sustaining. When Agnes wrote her mentor that Pope Gregory IX was pressuring her convent to abandon its call to poverty, Clare wrote poetically, "What you hold, may you hold. What you do, may you do and never abandon. But with swift pace, light step, unswerving feet, so that even your steps stir up no dust, may you go forward securely, joyfully, and swiftly, on the path to prudent happiness."[5] Clare's phrase "prudent happiness" shows that she knows how difficult—and how crucial—it is hear one's self, to listen to one's voice and to be comforted. Knowing that Agnes's soul was watered by prayer, Clare advised her to be resolute. Besides, Clare had had plenty of similar tussles with the church hierarchy, so she could empathetically encourage Agnes.

WORKING WOMEN'S WOES
Run-ins with church hierarchy was a constant theme for women

in the Middle Ages. As Hildegard and Clare knew from their own experience, some arguments were over lofty, theological matters, but other medieval women fought the church over more down-to-earth matters. For instance, in 1416, the prioress of Carrow Abbey in Norwich, England (where Julian may have been a nun prior to becoming an anchoress), took the prior of the cathedral and another monk to court for driving cattle from the convent's pastures to their own grazing lands.[6]

Margery wrote of her twenty-year struggle to get a scribe (typically, a member of the clergy) to inscribe as she dictated her book: "there was so much abuse and slander of this creature that few men would believe this creature."[7]

Even women who worked outdoors had their share of office politics. The husband-wife historian team of Frances and Joseph Gies write that a woman's working life in the Middle Ages was "hard and hazardous."[8] In the countryside, the poorest women (and men) searched for work such as making and stacking hay or caring for livestock. Rural women's work

> *was not merely service such as cooking and cleaning, but production and manufacture of the family's food and clothing. She milked the cows; soaked, beat and combed out the flax; fed the chickens, ducks and geese; sheared the sheep, made the cheese and butter; and cultivated the family vegetable patch. Sometimes she spun and wove to eke out a cash income. She also worked along with her husband outside—sowing, reaping, gleaning, binding, threshing, raking, winnowing, thatching. At times she even helped with the plowing, wielding the goad that drove the oxen while her husband gripped the handles of the plow.*[9]

Wives of householders did more indoor work, such as managing staff and keeping the books.

Like their rural sisters, city women worked for lower wages than men. Even the smallest town had a variety of skilled laborers: millers, barrel makers, butchers, carpenters, brewers, blacksmiths, tinsmiths, candle makers. Particularly in Italy and Flanders (which is now parts of Belgium, France, and the Netherlands), women participated in the textile industry. English city women were more likely to work as alewives or at making and selling charcoal—and they also sold fish, poultry, and meat.

Women were often excluded from the guilds that dominated medieval Europe and deprived of their benefits. Outside Paris in 1263, for instance, the bakers guild claimed women should not be allowed to make and sell bread because they weren't strong enough to knead dough. In some cases, women were admitted to the guilds, but this usually occurred, as you've probably guessed, when a husband or sometimes a father was a member. For instance, the pastry cooks guild of Poitiers, France, admitted wives, but, "Mistresses, when they are widows, can keep one or two workers, but they are permitted to carry only one single box of wafers through town." And only male members and their sons were allowed to attend the dinner welcoming new members. In some cases, especially in England, guilds sought to limit the employment of women. In 1344, the London girdlers (belt makers) resolved that wives and daughters of members were the only women they would hire.[10]

WORKING GIRLS: BARBARA BAESINGER FUGGER, MARGERY OF KEMPE, AND HADEWIJCH OF BRABANT

Despite the obstacles in their path, a few medieval single women were able to earn a good living. My favorite example is Barbara Baesinger Fugger of Augsburg, Germany. In 1469, she was widowed with eleven children. None of her sons was old enough to take over her husband's textile business, so she did, even expanding it. She trained two sons in the business and sent a third, Jacob, to Rome to study for the priesthood. In time, however, a number of Barbara's children died and Jacob was needed back in Augsburg, so Barbara called him home to help with the business, "and thereby introduced to the commercial stage the greatest businessman of the Middle Ages, 'Jacob the Rich' Fugger, whose loans to prelates and financing of the sale of benefices and indulgences played a big role in bringing on the Protestant Reformation."[11] Not only was Barbara brave and smart, she was also obviously a mentor.

Barbara is also a model for modern women who have stepped off their career path, or who never stepped on a typical one. In my own case as an Episcopal priest, that proscribed career path is working as the rector of progressively larger parishes. I found the 2006 election of Katharine Jefferts Schori as presiding bishop of the Episcopal Church to be a breath of fresh air in many ways—not the least of which because our new presiding bishop had not followed this career path. Before she was a priest, Jefferts Schori was an oceanographer and, once she was ordained, she didn't follow the typical church career path, bypassing the position of rector altogether.

Margery of Kempe knew all about the downside of business—two of her enterprises failed, a brewery and a mill. Both times, she was able to hear God in her struggle. She realized that her pride had gotten in the way of her business sense. In fact, she'd boasted about her faith to make others feel inadequate and took pleasure in making the neighbors envious, spending money that perhaps should have gone into the business lavishly on fine clothes and gold hairpins. She may also have realized that being in business for herself was not for her. (As my wise friend Anne once told me when I was having a painful time,

"You must be learning a lot because you're hurting a lot. They usually go hand in hand, you know.")

Hadewijch of Brabant (early thirteenth century) seems to have endured the sad demise of her career. What we know of her comes from her extensive writing, which indicates that she was well educated in subjects usually taught in schools for wealthy young men: rhetoric, numerology, astronomy, music theory, and theology, as well as Latin and French. Despite all her education, Hadewijch had an appetite for the Harlequin romances of her day: love poetry of chivalrous young men and virtuous young ladies. She took the love poems of her day as her wool, and wove them into love songs between the divine and seekers of faith. All in all, thirty-one letters, forty-five poems in stanzas, fourteen visions, and sixteen poems in couplets still exist from Hadewijch's body of work Hadewijch headed a group of Beguines, which she may have founded, and held the position for a number of years. Details are sketchy, but there was a mutiny, and Hadewijch was evicted from the community she had once led. Those who supported her were dispersed, and Hadewijch found herself homeless. At least one scholar has conjectured that Hadewijch used the skills she'd acquired as a Beguine, followed her own advice, and probably earned her living by caring for the sick and poor.[12]

That's a pretty sad picture for someone who took such obvious joy in her fellow Beguines. Hadewijch wrote about one who particularly inspired her, "She let everything happen without surprise and without complaint, and she loved no one unless she knew them to be in the being of love in heaven, on earth—the dead, the living, and those not yet born. Everything else, then, was all the same to her, as it is also for me now. Love made her grow up into the perfect essence of her being."[13] By Love, of course, Hadewijch refers to the divine. Hadewijch unfailingly gives God credit. She is one of those souls who teaches us that simply being grateful to God goes a long way toward drawing us closer to God, as well as to one another.

Hadewijch seems to have a knack for appreciating the gifts in people as well as in God. A fellow Beguine, Sara, struggled mightily with her spiritual life, even converting from Judaism to Christianity. At last, Sara found peace. Hadewijch writes, "After a time she came back to herself, and having received 74 lovely revelations and also the spirit of prophecy; she also had the true works of charity—something that surpasses all the rest. She had the Holy Spirit in her soul and in her body. With all her exercises (of virtue), she was a perfect mother of God."[14] Although it was a century before Meister Eckhart claimed that "God is always needing to be born," Hadewijch seems to have a similar intuition. In any case, Hadewijch admires Sara for her works of charity, which brought her peace.

Hadewijch even drew up a list of her spiritual heroes, which she titled "List of the Perfect." Perhaps controversy over who was, and wasn't, on the list, had something to do with Hadewijch's demise. In any case, the list consisted of eighty-six people, living and dead whom she considered to be "clothed in love." The image Hadewijch uses to determine inclusion on her list is a good reminder that being aware of God's proximity ("as close as our own clothing," as Julian of Norwich would say in the next century) translates into treating others, ourselves and the world, with love. Especially in Hadewijch's day, living out one's faith was not without its risks: among the names is a Beguine who was executed for her beliefs around 1236.

Of all Hadewijch's writings, the one I find most poignant is a letter to a young Beguine in which she wrote guardedly about her own experience of betrayal and then gave advice that perhaps she wished she had known enough to take. She wrote,

Now I want to warn you about one thing from which great harm can come. I assure you that this is one of the worst sicknesses which prevail today, and sicknesses there are plenty. Nowadays everyone is constantly questioning the good faith of his friends, putting them to the test and complaining of their faithlessness; and people spend their time in this way who ought to be filled with an exalted love for our great God.[15]

Given the reality of medieval office politics (as real for us in the twenty-first century as it was in the thirteenth), Hadewijch offered two main pieces of advice: "be on your guard against instability" and "never abandon the true life of good works."

Hadewijch seems to understand how easy it is to lose one's center, and how detrimental that can be to one's spirituality. She writes, "For there is nothing so able and so quick to separate you from our Lord as instability." As an antidote, she gives us a sort of mantra with a warning attached.

Whatever troubles may come to you, do not commit the folly of believing that you are set for any other goal than the great God Himself, in the fullness of His being and His love; do not let folly or doubt deflect you from any good practice which can lead you to this goal. If you will confide yourself to His love, you will soon grow to your full stature, but if you persist in doubting, you will become sluggish and grudging, and everything which you ought to do will be a burden to you. Let nothing trouble you [as Teresa of Avila will also advise three centuries later], do not believe that anything which you must do for Him whom you seek will be beyond your strength, that you cannot surmount it, that it will be beyond you. This is the fervor, this is the zeal which you must have, and all the time your strength must grow."

Midlife Careers, Then and Now

A recent study on middle-aged women points out that a frequent challenge to working is the basic, but frequently complex, work of creating a career path. "Work is a psychological balm for most midlife women," the summary reads.

> *Midlife women who are employed report better health, lower anxiety, less depression and greater subjective well-being than women who stay at home, studies find. That said, women's work histories are often erratic because of parenting and caretaking duties. . . . As a consequence, midlife women often lack sufficient money, and later, sufficient retirement funds. . . . Because midlife women are so diverse, significant in-group differences exist. While many midlife women are doing well, certain groups fare worse than others. . . . African-American women, for example, and midlife women in ill health may have a particularly tough time.*[16]

Despite her trials, or maybe because of them, Hadewijch is somehow able to cheer us on. Her writings encourage us to stay serenely focused on the prize of seeing God face-to-face for eternity, empowering us to do the work of Christ here on earth. Thankfully, not every one of us will be laid off, as Hadewijch was, or otherwise given reasons to be embittered about our work. But even the most fulfilling work is marked by ups and downs and patches of excessive stress or tedium. Hadewijch teaches us that when you invite Jesus to use your work to support the work of God, your perspective will change. Your broadened point of view will enable you to ride the waves of work better, even when those waves include the sea change of retirement. And your enlarged focus will give you a deeper sense of reward than any paycheck ever could.

Our mystics present us with varied career models: Hadewijch, who battled bitterness, Hildegard and Clare, who persevered in mentoring; Barbara, who ignored convention. But as different as they are from each other, all of these women stress that careers, and every aspect of our lives, must be founded on a love of God if we are to find meaning in our work.

A PRAYER TO GET STARTED

O God who is as comfortable in the boardroom as in the living room, and whose love for us transcends all the circumstances of our lives, thank you for the opportunities of this life. Thank you for our abilities to be inspired and to inspire others. Thank you for endowing each of us with unique gifts. Thank you for providing ways we can offer our gifts to the world. Endow us with wisdom to navigate the wider world in which we work. Endow us with patience and confidence so that our work may glorify you. Make our work please you, and serve the world that you have created. In the name of you, whom Hadewijch teaches us clothes us in your love, Amen.

QUESTIONS FOR JOURNALING AND REFLECTION

1. Let Hadewijch's "List of the Perfect" inspire you. Who are your heroes? Hadewijch listed eighty-six people, living and dead, who showed that they were clothed in God's love. How many are on your list? And why are they there? Say a prayer for each of them, and let their examples inspire your own life.

2. You've probably seen the poster I refer to on leadership and geese. Dhuoda of Septimania points to stags as a good example of leadership. What animals inspire you, and why?

3. Hadewijch understood our tendency to forget that we are "clothed in love," as she said, even when challenges overwhelm us. Do you agree with her that "We deny love her

rightful place in the valleys of life"?[17] Next time you're in the valleys of shadow, remind yourself that the Shepherd is with you. You may want to consider making this reminder a constant habit.

4. Recall mentors in your life—older moms on the playground, a really good boss, a teacher who inspired you. Now write at least one of them a thank-you note. And say a prayer for the rest. Don't forget to include a prayer for the young women you mentor.

11

A ROOM OF YOUR OWN

I admit it. I was a nosy babysitter. Once I'd put my charges to bed, nothing was sacred. I'd leaf through wedding albums, take stock of record collections, judge my employers by the magazines to which they subscribed and the canned goods in their cupboards. I didn't open drawers or read mail (my mother's admonitions rang loudly in my mind), but I did occasionally stray from the living room to open doors to rooms I had no need to enter. Usually, this meant the master bedroom, and no sooner would I catch a glimpse of my guilty self in a dresser mirror than I would skedaddle back to the living room couch. But once, I opened a narrow door from a master bedroom that led to a freshly painted set of stairs and a tiny room. There was a single bed, neatly made, and a nightstand with a reading lamp and a notebook on it. That was it. I gave in to the dark side of curiosity, opened the journal, and started to read.

My employer, a mild-mannered stay-at-home mom, wrote about needing "a room of one's own" to save her sanity. She probably wrote about many other things, but perhaps because

I read her diary as I stood in her private sanctuary, the message has never left me. It was probably sometime in college when I learned that my employer didn't invent that phrase. It was a woman named Virginia Woolf, and "A Room of One's Own" is the title of an essay she published in 1929. Noting the paucity of fiction about women written by women, Woolf claimed that a woman needs a steady income and a room of her own to write.

Harper Lee wrote the bulk of *To Kill a Mockingbird* after receiving a Christmas gift from friends in the form of a note that read, "You have one year off from your job to write whatever you please. Merry Christmas." That was 1956. Within a year, Lee had completed a first draft of *To Kill a Mockingbird*. When Lee's novel was published in 1960, it was an overnight sensation and was voted "Best Novel of the Century" in a 1999 poll conducted by *Library Journal*. Although none of our mystics articulated this need for "a room of one's own" as memorably as Woolf, their cheers ring across the centuries.

FINDING SOLITUDE IN THE MIDDLE AGES

It's a shame that Woolf apparently never came across the work of Hrosvit (c. 935–c. 1002), the Saxon playwright whose work is noteworthy for its portrayal of women as strong and rational. Frequently, her female characters are prophetic agents of salvation. Traditional feminine traits such as compassion and traditional male traits such as reason abide harmoniously in Hrosvit's female heroes. Contemporary scholar and fellow Benedictine Sister Teresa Wolking reminds us that Hrosvit was blessed by the resources of Gandersheim, the convent where she lived—and where intellectualism was highly valued. "Exhibiting sympathy, compassion, understanding, [she] balances with feminine traits all the abstract masculine thought processes learned from her classical training."[1]

One of Woolf's most enthusiastic heavenly cheerleaders

was surely Teresa of Avila. As scholar Carol Lee Flinders notes,

> *Roughly four hundred years before Virginia Woolf wrote "A Room of One's Own," which maintained that women would certainly prove the equal of men in creativity once they had the privilege of doors they could close, Teresa of Avila insisted in her "Rule" that every nun should have a cell that no one could enter without permission. . . . She defended as god-given her spiritual daughters' right to inwardness itself—and to living situations, mentors and books that facilitated it—because nothing else would permit the "still small voice" from within to be heard.*[2]

I imagine Catherine of Siena also encouraged Woolf from heaven. The teenaged Catherine was what your mother would have called "a handful." At one point, she cut her lustrous locks to spite her parents, who wanted her to marry. As a punishment, upper-crust Catherine was made to perform menial work in the household, and her family, knowing she craved solitude, never allowed her to be alone. Years later, she wrote in *The Dialogue* that in the middle of this trial, God had shown her how to build in her soul a private cell where no tribulation could enter.[3]

Nancy Murray, a Dominican nun who travels around the world portraying Catherine in a one-woman show, notes the courage it takes to construct a room inside one's soul. According to Sister Nancy, Catherine "would say, 'Stand up, don't be afraid.' That's something she said often. She would say we need to bridge evil with goodness and be part of the healing, draw from our own well of prayer, respond with compassion and be faithful to God's word." Drawing from that inner well allowed Catherine to be the complex person she was. "She was sassy. She was funny. She was feisty, but lovable; direct, but gentle. She knew the power of God's love."

Catherine grew from a confused teenager into a poised, powerful woman who stressed the importance of speaking out against injustice. Sister Nancy paraphrases from Catherine's letter that resonates most strongly with her: "No more silence! Shout with a hundred thousand tongues! I am seeing the world going to ruin because people are not speaking out."[4]

Catherine of Siena's contemporary, Julian of Norwich, took things a step beyond an inner cell and went so far as to be enclosed in a physical room of her own. In a sense, of course, Julian withdrew from the world (in fact, the word anchorite comes from the Greek for "I withdraw"), but in a larger sense, she simply ordered her world so she could be more profoundly engaged with it. In the first place, Julian didn't become a hermit—as an anchoress, she was allowed to have a helper to provide food and so on, as well a cat for company in her cell (a cow being deemed too cumbersome).[5] In the second place, she was on call to the world outside her window. Julian expert Sarah Law writes, "I am sure that Julian's life was the longer and her psyche was the stronger because of her balanced approach."[6]

Julian was esteemed enough to be left provisions in several wills, and Margery Kempe, who sought spiritual advice from Julian, found her to be patient and empathetic. Margery, who had her share of emotional and spiritual struggles, wrote of her visit with Julian, "I was able to tell her of the grace that God had put into my soul; of my compunction for past sins, of my contrition, the consolations I received from my devotions."[7]

Julian's life models for us that we should not retreat from the world, but make room for ourselves so that we can offer our authentic selves to the world. Likewise, Catherine of Siena, in stressing the need for an inner cell, compared this process of discovering ourselves for the sake of being more Christlike in the world to the way damp logs burn. She wrote,

> *Truly the soul's being united with and transformed into him is like fire consuming the dampness in logs. Once the logs are heated through and through, the fire burns and changes them into itself, giving them its own color and warmth and power. It is just so with us when we look at our Creator and his boundless charity. We begin to experience the heat of self-knowledge—which consumes all the dampness of our selfish love for ourselves. As the heat increases, we throw ourselves with blazing desire into God's measureless goodness, which we discover within our very selves. We are then sharing in his warmth and in his power, in that we begin at once to feed on and savor souls.*[8]

Hopeful, isn't it, that as we know ourselves more deeply, we're better able to love others as well as ourselves?

DOWN TIME, THEN AND NOW

One of the most rewarding things you can learn about yourself is how you desire to offer yourself to the world. As for myself, I was the youngest grandchild on both sides, and both sets of grandparents lived nearby, so I was frequently taken by doting grandparents to visit with their siblings and other relatives. To this day, I treasure a photo of my three-year-old self surrounded by my Grandma and Grandpa Jackson, Aunt Lizzie, and Uncle Herman. I'm seated on a bench between Grandma and hersister, and their husbands stand behind them in their overalls. The picture stays on the bulletin board above my desk, and looking at the wrinkled, loving faces of these four long-deceased souls gives me confidence as I work. No wonder I've always been so comfortable with older people, and look forward to visiting them in hospitals and nursing homes. My grandparents gave me a gift in my early childhood that translates into enjoying ministry with seniors today.

What about you? Do you engage in after-school tutoring because you always loved school? Did surviving an abusive marriage enable you to work with battered women? Maybe a neighbor whose kitchen always smelled of chocolate chip cookies or apple crisp has translated into your abilities as a hostess who makes everyone feel at home. No matter how you get to know yourself—journaling (thankfully you're beyond the point where you need to hide your diary from snooping babysitters!), therapy, long talks, or e-mails with a friend, persistent prayer—making room for yourself will also open avenues into your soul that can be offered to the world. Today's society rarely encourages reflection. We're rewarded for keeping busy, multitasking, and brimful calendars, but of course, we're human beings, not human doings. It can help to remind yourself that spending time in the room of your own soul leads to knowing yourself better, and the better you know yourself, the more authentic your service to others will be.

Law writes,

> *Prayer and meditation can open us to states of consciousness which are receptive to spirituality and to creative inspiration. In 1902, psychologist William James described this state as the "subliminal realm," a part of the psyche that is sensitive to imagery and receptive to grace. Today we might use the idea of left-brain/right-brain thinking. A recent book on Julianx describes her as very much a right-brain person, somebody who processes and makes sense of his or her experiences creatively and intuitively. And this puts us in touch with something larger than ourselves, however we wish to describe it. As priest and Jungian therapist Morton Kelsey puts it: "Each of us becomes the artist as we allow ourselves to*

be open to the reality of the Other and give expression to that encounter either in words or paint or stone or in the fabric of our lives. Each of us who has come to know and relate to the Other and expresses this in any way is an artist in spite of himself/herself."[9]

Author and Episcopal priest Barbara Cawthorne Crafton points out that even Jesus needed "quiet time" with God. Referring to Mark 1:35, "In the morning, while it was still very dark, he got up and went to a deserted place, and there he prayed," she writes, "we all need time to be alone with God. God needs to get a word in edgewise, and we're so busy and so noisy that he usually can't. But I have so little time to myself, we protest: *I can't add one more thing to my day, not one, and you want me to pray, too?* But prayer," Crafton insists, "isn't something you add to your day. It doesn't go on top of everything else; it goes on the bottom. It supports the other things you have on your plate, all of them. The time you spend in quiet prayer—and that included saying absolutely nothing at all, just letting God sit with you in silence—multiplies the value of all your other time. It puts things in perspective, helps you see the bigger picture of your life, to distinguish between the important and the merely urgent. Allows things to occur to you that you hadn't considered before."[10]

THE GREENING OF CREATIVITY: HILDEGARD OF BINGEN

Regular "quiet time" with God may well have contributed to Hildegard of Bingen's unrivaled creativity. She stands out for me as the most extraordinary example of a person whose creativity flowers from a deep, abiding relationship with God. Perhaps because she was such a creative, visual person, Hildegard came to write about the creativity of God in terms of a color. Skim

Hildegard's work and you'll find she wrote frequently of *viriditas*, probably a term she coined herself, which is usually translated as "greening." New Zealand biblical scholar David Crawley found himself excited about *viriditas* when he discovered one of Hildegard's songs in which she praises the greenness of God's finger. He understands *viriditas* thus:

> *God breathed* viriditas *into Adam and Eve at their creation. It fills the season of spring and "causes the grasses to laugh with the joy of life." Yet* viriditas *is equally the Spirit of God at work in us bringing spiritual life and renewal. "Greening" was her way of speaking about the creativity and fruitfulness of a human being fully alive and in harmony with the purposes of God.*[11]

No matter what the weather, Hildegard sees the world as greening, vibrantly brimming with creativity and love and activity.

Furthermore, Crawley writes, "I find myself inspired and encouraged by the way Hildegard gives prominence to this green-fingeredness of God. . . . Focusing on *viriditas* invites openness and trust, rather than striving and anxiety. We may plant and water, but only God can give the growth. Hildegard's own explosion of creativity in her early forties is an encouragement in itself, and a vivid outworking of *viriditas*. I say that not only because I am forty-something, but because her life powerfully demonstrates how the greening principle will persevere in finding ways to express itself, even when conditions are far from hospitable."[12]

One way Hildegard used the color green was by applying it to the Virgin Mary, whom she referred to as the *viridissima virga* (my rough translation is "the virgin who is the greening of all greening"). Historian Deborah Vass explains that Mary, as the Mother of God, possesses what Hildegard considers a "greening" role. As Mary gives life to all humans via the life she gave to Christ, we human beings also have *viriditas*. In gratitude for our viriditas, we human beings are called to co-create with God, cultivating the earthly and thereby creating the heavenly.[13]

Hildegard's energies were sapped by disputes with popes, bishops, priests, and monks—and the skirmishes were exacerbated by her insistence that medieval clergy—notoriously corrupt, frequently illiterate and often greedy—the clergy needed to clean up their act. Yet Hildegard insisted fiercely that God is present, that "greening" is ever available to every one of us.

TAKING HER TIME : MECTHILD OF HACKEBORN

In ways that are as unique as they are, each of our mystics constructed a room of her own. Mechthild of Hackeborn (c. 1240–1298) took her time in finding her own room, in which she began to write around her fiftieth birthday. My hunch is that Mechthild had a lot of growing up to do. In the first place, she had to overcome her knack for making herself the center of attention. At her birth, sometime in 1240 or 1241, into a noble family in what is now east-central Germany, Mechthild wasn't expected to live, so she was whooshed to the closest baptismal font, leaving the ancestral castle where she was born in an uproar. At the church, the infant caused another commotion, as her arrival delayed the priest saying Mass. The cleric wasn't fooled for a minute that the baptism was an emergency, chiding the midwives, "What do you fear? This child most certainly will not die, but she will become a saintly religious in whom God will work many wonders, and she will end her days in a good old age."

As a young girl, Mechthild was taken to visit her older sister, Gertrude of Hackeborn, and apparently immediately decided the cloistered life was the life for her. Tiring of her unrelenting whining, Mechthild's parents gave in and let her enter a convent, where she became the *domna cantrix*, the one who determined when the singing of each service was finished. All ears were on Mechthild.

Despite Mechthild's irritating need to be the center of attention (her beautiful singing voice helped), she enjoyed a particularly rich prayer life, and others noticed. (Maybe Mechthild let it slip that Jesus called her "Nightingale.") The other sisters tried to sweet-talk Mechthild into writing a book of her revelations, and she finally stopped playing coy when Jesus himself appeared to her, holding the book of her revelations and saying: "All this has been committed to writing by my will and inspiration; and, therefore you have no cause to be troubled about it." Mechthild's response was: "I cannot, nor do I wish to write, except that I see it with the eyes of my soul, and hear it with the ears of my external spirit and feel it in the members of my body: the power of the Holy Spirit."

Despite her youthful tendency to make sure everything was all about her, the mature Mechthild came to be respected as a spiritual guide to her fellow sisters as well as to clergy and lay people. She's given partial credit for developing the cult of the Sacred Heart of Jesus, in which scholar Jennifer Ward explains, "His heart was seen as a refuge and dwelling place, as when Christ, speaking to Mechthild of Hackeborn, likened his heart to a kitchen, the space in the house which was open to all."[14] I love that image of Jesus' heart as the space in the house open to all, especially since all the best parties end up in the kitchen. And I love Mechthild for sharing it with us. Although she doesn't seem to have been an easy personality, Mechthild seems to have overcome her touch of prima donna-itis by finding a room of her own. I have Mechthild's inner cell wasn't always a comfortable place. She had to come to terms with her personality traits that others found so abrasive, and that probably caused her deep loneliness. Yet, as she found her own space and began writing, Mechthild's creative expression was surely an enormous relief to her, as well as an offering to those around her.

I can understand our mystics' need for space—I've seen it time and again in my own life and ministry. I had a crotchety parishioner once whose stubborn insistence on God's love inspired me despite her prickly personality. Lily, as I'll call her, was a wealthy woman, and she was suffering by anyone's standards. She lay in a hospital bed for several weeks, knowing that this bed was likely to be her last. The nurses tried to control the pain as cancer ravaged her body, but Lily wasn't one of their favorite patients. She was demanding, sharp, and her usual mood was negative. Lily's room was devoid of flowers and held only a couple of cards—her husband had left her years earlier for another woman, and their children were scattered. Worse, they were estranged from her, from their father, and from each other. "That's the down side of money, dear," Lily whispered. "It can make things very lonely."

"Lily," I asked, "how do you cope with the loneliness in this hospital?" "Look up," she commanded, and so I did. "What do you see?" "Nothing special. It's just one of those suspended tile ceilings you always see in hospitals." "Humph!" snorted Lily. "There are crosses everywhere those pieces of metal meet. All you have to do is focus on one to remind yourself that Jesus is always with you."

I haven't looked at those ugly ceilings the same way since. Lily's right—there are crosses everywhere, and so are there reminders of God's presence. Catherine of Siena put it beautiful-ly, in a prayer in which she asked for a complete realization of God's presence, for "There the soul dwells—like the fish in the sea and the sea in the fish."[15]

If we are to swim in God's love, so to speak, Catherine suggests that we have to find a way outside ourselves—outside the isolation navel gazing brings. We need to claim our "inner cell," our room of our own, inside the endless realm of God's love, and ask to be released from ourselves. We need to trust that God has given us all we need to contribute to the world, and to contribute it with confidence. It may not always be easy, but we can always ask for help, for God always longs to "come back to the soul to fill her with . . . blessedness." And the reward for this trust is a kind of lightness that enables us to live in the world while knowing that, as a fish exists in water, we swim in God.

A PRAYER TO GET STARTED

O God who longs to meet me in the quiet, private moments of my life, and who created the inner cells of my soul, thank you for the holy place in me that is known only to you. Help me to see my inner cell as an open, fertile place that offers my soul deep nourishment. Help me to remember that my inner cell is always available, and that you are always ready to meet me there. Thank you for the women who have gone before me who insisted on having a room of their own. Help me to respect my inner life and to give it the attention I deserve. Help me to respect the space that others need. In the name of you, in whom Catherine reminds us we live like the fish in the sea, and the sea in the fish, Amen.

QUESTIONS FOR JOURNALING AND REFLECTION

1. Mechthild of Hackeborn made an extraordinary journey in her life from self-centeredness toward self-giving. What has your journey been like thus far? What kind of path would you like to travel? Mechthild took a significant turn at age fifty when she began writing. How have significant turns in your life manifested themselves creatively? What creative urges do you intend to act on in the next years of your life?

2. What makes it hard for you to spend time in your inner cell? Is it time? Is it other people? Is it space? It is yourself? How could your life, and you, change if you respected your inner cell?

3. Spend a little time thinking about the heart of Jesus. How do you think of Jesus' heart? Does the metaphor of Jesus' heart as a kitchen resonate with you? Does the heart of Jesus have anything in common with your inner cell?

4. My former parishioner, Lily, was anything but an easy person to be near, and yet her finding the literal cross in the depths of her ordeal inspired me. Have you ever known anyone in the midst of a trial who has been able to encourage you?

12

DEATH: YOU MIGHT AS WELL THINK ABOUT IT WHILE THERE'S STILL TIME

Eleanor Roosevelt had the right idea. She once wrote, "Long ago I made up my mind that the one thing that made life worth while was to live as fully as possible. There are so many years to be dead."[1]

Perhaps people of no other era in western history were as death-obsessed—as aware of the many years to be dead—as were those who lived in the Middle Ages. These centuries have the reputation for being bloody and bawdy—life was so expendable that people scarcely had time to grieve, and hellfire and damnation awaited nearly everyone. Even little kids apparently understand the Middle Ages as a perpetual Halloween, a time when this world and the next were both scary places.

When my son Ted turned seven, he wanted a "castle times" party, having outgrown dinosaurs and pirates. Ted and his friends smeared sugar cubes with icing "glue" to make their own castles, but the highlight of the party was clearly when each guest was "dubbed" with a plastic sword before going home with more sugar in their little bellies than in their hands. Apparently, violence and gore—barbarians and torture, boiling oil and armored combat, and brushes with death—fascinated these deceptively angelic-looking first-graders.

The Getty Museum of Los Angeles, much more sophisticated than any first-grader I've ever met, recently held an exhibition entitled "Images of Violence in the Medieval World," a tribute to "[medieval] people [being] surrounded by violence in many forms, including wars, brutal tournaments, and deadly rivalries for power and land. Graphic depictions of violent religious events, such as Christ's Crucifixion," the curators note, "were also common."[2]

The Meaning of Medieval Death

Yet perhaps because early deaths and gruesome diseases were everyday events in "castle times," our mystics stressed the *love* and not the wrath of God, which permeates our existence in this life and the next, perhaps in response to the everyday roughness and frequent cruelty of the era. In fact, a French monk, Bernard of Clairvaux (1090–1153), is often credited with insisting on a kinder, gentler world view.

Bernard was a sort of twelfth-century Martin Luther. Like Luther, Bernard was a reformer, criticizing his fellow Benedictines for letting their simple, devotional lives get out of balance: worship had become elaborate and rite laden, and both meditation and manual labor had gone by the wayside. Bernard's criticism could be acerbic—he once accused the pope of foolishly laboring over church politics, asking, "What does it yield you in the end but cobwebs?"[3] Nevertheless, it's hard to imagine the Jesus Bernard knew as anything other than sympathetic. Although most male preachers (and most of the preachers were male) throughout the Middle Ages likened Jesus to a harsh judge or an absolute, unforgiving monarch, Bernard compared Jesus to an attentive lover. He interpreted the Hebrew love sonnet known as the Song of Songs[4] as an intimate conversation between Christ and his church, or between Christ and his beloved—and that beloved is anyone who follows him. Because at face value the poem celebrates erotic love between a bride and groom, it was easy enough to read the work as a personal love song between Christ and a woman follower—although it was written well before Christ's birth.

To be sure, Bernard had another side to him—he also preached in favor of the Second Crusade. Crusades (and indulgences) were so popular in part because of the medieval fear of what awaited in death. Fighting for Christ, or buying time off purgatory for yourself or for loved ones were sort of insurance policies to mitigate eternity. Given this mindset, it's not hard to understand that when the Muslims declared victory (the Second Crusade was a disaster for the Christians), Bernard blamed the loss on the Christian crusaders' sins. Although I've read several scholars who comment on Bernard's impact on the people of his time, including several of our mystics, I think it's a big leap to claim that women who lived so far away from (and in many cases, so far after) Bernard were deeply influenced by him. Bernard preached long before the age of instant communication, and the roads medieval messengers trod were notoriously dangerous. Though Bernard's preaching that Christ loves us intimately and individually would strike a chord with medieval women mystics, it's unlikely that many of them would have known of his sermons. One exception could have been Hildegard, because her life overlapped with Bernard's and we know he read the first few chapters of her work, *Scivias*.[5]

In any case, our mystics were uniformly gentle with the bereaved, which gives me hope that grief-stricken people in medieval times heard tender voices alongside the harsh booming about judgment that ended in being swallowed by the mouth of hell, to endure eternal punishment. Perhaps death had a just-around-the-corner quality in the Middle Ages because disease, childbirth, and accidents were more lethal (and because the practices that sanitize death hadn't been invented yet), but I cannot believe that bereavement was any less painful then than now.

GROWTH THROUGH GRIEF: BEATRICE OF NAZARETH

Although medieval women were considered property of their fathers, Beatrice of Nazareth was blessed with supportive parents, who were wealthy merchants outside Brussels. Her mother, Gertrude, was by all accounts loving, but died when Beatrice, the youngest of six children, was around seven years old. Beatrice was fortunate that her father, Barthelomeus, did not resent paying the fees to beguniages and abbeys to have his bright young daughter educated. In fact, Bathelomeus had founded one of the convents where his daughter was schooled. Apparently, Beatrice enjoyed learning, but her grief for her mother led to deep depression. Around age fifteen, Beatrice took vows to become a nun, and her visions began two years later.

Over time, Beatrice's depression lifted as her visions increased. Her visions continued for the rest of her life, and were marked by the twin convictions that knowledge of God comes through love of neighbor, and that love of neighbor comes through the knowledge of God. In other words, we need to be both a Mary and Martha (see Luke 10:38-42), bringing both action and reflection to our spiritual lives in order to achieve wholeness. We need to be like Martha, productive and living out our faith, and like Mary, taking time to reflect.

Landing on a way to be both reflective and giving, Beatrice became expert at manuscript writing and illumination. She also helped found two monasteries, one of which she'd asked her father to fund. Eventually, Beatrice became prioress of this monastery outside Antwerp, Our Lady of Nazareth. Despite her administrative duties, she found time to write prolifically in both Latin and the vernacular Middle Dutch. At first, her writing was mostly a well-kept journal, but it evolved into advice for her fellow nuns at Nazareth as well as for all Christians. The only extant manuscript from Beatrice's body of work is *On Seven Ways of Holy Love*, which she penned around her fortieth birthday. In it she claims that *anyone*, not just cloistered nuns, can come to a deeply satisfying relationship with God.

Beatrice's work reminds me a bit of twelve-step programs, because each stage builds on the previous one. However, Beatrice is less concerned with accomplishment, with "curing" feelings of detachment from God, than with the stages of God's drawing us toward a sort of God-magnet, made easier if we keep ourselves open to the divine. In the first stage, you start to notice a sort of tickle from God. Next comes making room for God in your life, which involves a sort of cleaning to rid yourself of "impediment from the past, with a free consciousness and with pure spirit and a clear mind." Beatrice moves in her mourning toward God, adding courage, perseverance and service to others to her grief. Eventually, she finds her soul at a balancing point. Writing of herself in the third person, Beatrice writes, "And then she is like a housewife who has well taken care of her house, who has furnished it in a clever way and who has put it in order nicely, who protects it wisely, who guards it cleverly, and who works according to her plan. She brings inside [prayer and reflection] and outside [the tasks of love]."[6] This involves practice of course, but as her grief matures, she is in sync with both her pain and her joy, with both her God and herself. Beatrice has found gifts in grief, and so can you.

NEAR-DEATH EXPERIENCE

Julian of Norwich is a logical mystic to turn to in bereavement, because, in a sense, she knew about death from the other side of it. In the first place, her revelations came to her when she was so close to death she reported having been aware of her grieving mother moving to close her eyes. In the second place, when anyone became an anchoress or an anchorite in medieval England, they underwent rites conducted by a bishop that were written to echo the Mass for the dead. Julian was anointed by the bishop as if he were anointing a corpse, and the door leading from the church to her cell was sealed firmly shut—she probably heard the bishop proclaim her "dead to the world." Her punishment for renouncing her vows as an anchoress would have been permanent excommunication.

Julian stressed that any wrath we think is coming from God is actually coming from ourselves. God is all about forgiveness. "And this [God's forgiveness] is the highest joy that the soul understood," she wrote, continuing, "[M]y sin will not impede the operation of his goodness . . . and as we come to heaven each one of us will see it with wonderful joy; and it will go on operating until the last day. And the honor and bliss of it will last in heaven before God and all his holy saints eternally."[7] You can imagine what a relief it must have been to stop by Julian's window on the world and be assured that no matter how grave your loved one's sins, eternal love would be the reward.

Like Julian, Catherine of Siena had a near-death experience. In her mid-twenties, Catherine apparently stopped breathing for four hours, and some witnesses thought she'd died. Later, Catherine could never discuss the event without bursting into tears. Flinders tells the story thus:

> *Sometime before 1373, [Catherine] gave every appear-*
> *ance of having died. For four hours, according to many*

*witnesses, she stopped breathing. She had felt fully unit-
ed with God. Despite her protests, Jesus sent her back to
her body, promising that she would bring blessings to
many, and that so long as she carried out His work, she
would feel his presence. He would be with her.*

*For a long time before this she had been in an ecstatic
state, and at last she began to pray continuously to be
taken "from this body of death," and fully united with
God. "I did not obtain this," she told [a friend] later,
"but I did finally manage to get Him to communicate
the pains that He had felt to me, in so far as I was able
to hear them."... But to her anguish, the Lord sent her
back into the body. "For the good of souls," she had to
return to the world. "I shall be with you always," her
Beloved promised, but she must carry out his work....
"I saw the hidden things of God," she would recall, "and
now I am thrust back into the prison of the body."*[8]

The only possible conclusion Catherine's witness leaves us
with is that something far, far better than what we know awaits
us after death.

Beatrice is a particularly comforting mystic, especially if the
one whose death grieves you was a person of faith or someone
who suffered a great deal. Beatrice wrote of such a person:

*[T]he earth is a great misery to her, and a tough prison
and a heavy sorrow.... The earth has become a burden
to her and what belongs to the earth cannot satisfy or
content her.... Love has dragged her on and has led her
and taught her to go her way. This she has followed
faithfully, often with a lot of trouble and effort... Dead
or alive she wants to belong to love.... he wants to*

*follow love, experience love and enjoy love, and this
cannot happen to her in this misery. . . . [In heaven], the
soul is with her Groom and she becomes totally one
spirit with Him, in inseparable loyalty and in mutual
love for ever. . . . May God bring us all to that.*[9]

Even Catherine of Genoa, who insisted that purgatory exists
(as did most of her contemporaries), offers comfort. Your loved
ones may undergo purgatory, but it is intended to be more of a
preparation for heaven than a punishment. "[I]n this purification,
what is obliterated and cast out is not the soul, one with God, but
the lesser self. Having come to the point of twenty-four carats,
gold cannot be purified any further; and this is what happens to
the soul in the fire of God's love."[10] In fact, Catherine claimed,

*There is no joy save that in paradise to be compared to
the joy of the souls in purgatory. This joy increases day
by day because of the way in which the love of God
corresponds to that of the soul, since the impediment to
that love is worn away daily. This impediment is the
rust of sin. As it is consumed the soul is more and more
open to God's love.*[11]

So not even purgatory is so bad. You can take comfort in
knowing that your loved ones are truly in a better place—better because they know God on a deeper level than possible in
this life.

LOVE AND DEATH, THEN AND NOW
Henri Nouwen, in many ways a contemporary mystic, wrote,

*Death or absence does not end or even diminish the love
of God that brought you to the other person. It calls you*

*to take a new step into the mystery of God's inex-
haustible love. This process is painful, very painful,
because the other person has become a true revelation of
God's love for you. But the more you are stripped of the
God-given support of people, the more you are called to
love God for God's sake. This is an awesome and even
dreadful love, but it is the love that offers eternal life.*[12]

None of us, of course, escapes death, and part of midlife for
many of us is the realization that we've lived half our lives already.
The medieval people who survived outbreaks of the plague must
have been especially aware of life's fleeting quality. Playwrights
and painters of the fourteenth and fifteenth centuries created a
motif called "The Dance of Death" as reminders that death
comes to everyone. In the plays, which popped up especially in
Germany and Spain, characters portraying the dead often warned
the living something along the lines of "You are what we were;
you'll be what we are." Paintings on the theme were especially
popular among French artists, but the greatest example of the
genre comes from Lubeck in what is now northern German.
Only a copy of the original "Totentanz," dating from 1463, exists
today, in Estonia. The painting was designed almost like a comic
strip to show that death is the ultimate equalizer, coming to
popes, peasants, and everyone—empresses, maidens, even
babies—in between. One reason this particular depiction of the
Dance of Death is so popular is that the skeletons leading the living to their graves are so, well, lively. They're gleeful and gruesome, while the living are stiff and serious and static.

VISION OF DEATH: MARGUERITE PORETE

Few of us find the prospect of our own death a laughing matter,
though we may attempt to cover that fear with jokes or nervous

titters. Probably because their visions frequently gave them windows on eternity, our mystics seemed to have put the fear of death behind them—including Marguerite Porete (c. 1280–1310). Although she spent a year and a half in prison before she was burned at the stake in Paris for heresy, Marguerite refused to apologize for anything in *The Mirror of Simple Souls*, which she had written sometime between 1296 and 1306. The book, practically all sixty thousand words of it (that would translate to about 240 pages of typed manuscript), is a conversation between Reason, Love, and the Soul. Like Beatrice, who wrote of seven stages that bring us deeper to God's love, Marguerite also wrote of seven stages of grace. While Beatrice was concerned with our relationship with God in this life, Marguerite's seven stages cross over between this world and the next.

The first step is to obey God's commandments; the next, to follow Jesus' example. The third step is to put others before self, which enables one to enter the fourth stage of deep prayer. Stage five is one of pure humility so that in the next step, the soul can be completely cleansed and free of sin. Stage seven is perfection, and that can be reached only after death. No matter which step we stand on, Marguerite told us that "God is to be found, and [the soul] finds God within itself without even looking."[13] Perhaps that is heaven's greatest gift: the certainty that God is in us without even looking, as Marguerite said; or that the soul dwells in God as the fish in the sea and the sea in the fish, as Catherine of Siena put it; or that God is our very breath, as Julian saw it.

While none of our mystics devalued this life, all of them agreed that the life to come is far superior to our current existence. Catherine of Siena viewed our time on this earth as a sort of blink of God's eye. "All suffering in this life is small with the smallness of time," she claimed. "Time is no more than the point of a needle, and when time is over, so is suffering."[14] Although it's hard for us keep this life in the eternal perspective, it's comforting to remember that suffering ends when we leave this realm of time and space for eternity.

Perhaps because of her near-death experience, Catherine of Siena envisioned Jesus as a bridge between this life and the next. Along the way, Jesus provides us with "inns" where we receive nourishment and rest to complete our earthly journeys, and to prepare us for the next life. Nobody's claiming this world is easy—or even that leaving it is a piece of cake. But what our mystics *did* claim is that you don't have to go it alone in this life or in the next. Hildegard wrote, "Man contains the entire creation within himself, and the breath of life that never dies is within him. . . . Even when our eternal eyes are closed, the soul . . . already knows it can live without the body."[15]

The Thanksgiving morning my husband and I were battling cancer, he woke me to tell me about a dream he'd just awakened from. "This man I didn't know, really, except that somehow I'd known him all my life, came into this room and promised he would take my pain away." We agreed that Scott must have dreamed of Jesus, who was promising to cure him. The cure didn't come the way we'd so desperately hoped and prayed for, but I believe Jesus did indeed come. The next June, as we slept in the same bed where Scott had had the dream, Scott died, and I've come to believe that Jesus took Scott's pain away as he took him to heaven.

When people ask me about grief, I tell them that while I don't find that the pain eases, I do find that one can become stronger in living with the pain. Grief is like a dinner guest who never leaves, but one for whom you can eventually find room for at the table where you live your life. I think it's that way with your own mortality, as well. For most of us, it takes losing someone we love to come to terms with the fact that we, too, shall die. Thankfully, there's room at your table for both your grief and your own mortality. I find it's easier when I let those who've loved me—and our mystics—pull up chairs as well.

Many of us find that child and work duties ease as we age, leaving us more time for reflection. This can be a frightening prospect, particularly if you haven't spent much time in your inner cell. And yet, now can be the time to give, or ask for, forgiveness; to remind people that you love them; to say "thank you"; to leave behind whatever you want people to use to remember you. With your heightened sense of mortality, you can make more purposeful choices about your life. Fred "Mister" Rogers put it this way: "In the eternal scheme of things, shining moments are as brief as the twinkling of an eye, yet such twinklings are what eternity is made of—moments when we human beings can say, 'I love you,' 'I'm proud of you,' 'I forgive you,' 'I'm grateful for you.' That's what eternity is made of: invisible, imperishable *good stuff*."[16]

Although Julian allowed that we shall "still be longing for love" on the day we die, she saw eternity as holding deep satisfaction on all levels. "[W]e shall all come into our Lord, knowing ourselves clearly and wholly possessing God, and we shall all be endlessly hidden in God, truly seeing and wholly feeling, and hearing him. . . . And there we shall see God face to face, familiarly and wholly." We'll also have deep insight into ourselves that will help us love God, and presumably those we love, better. "And when we know and see, truly and clearly, what our self is, then we shall truly and clearly see and know our Lord God in the fullness of joy."[17]

Julian's insight is a lovely lesson for middle age. It is never too late to know yourself better, and it is always worth the trouble, not only for yourself, but for your relationship with God and with others. In their words and in their lives, all our mystics pointed out that part of maturity is a growing certainty that God loves you. Loves your shortcomings, loves everything that is unique about you, loves you through the journey that is your life. And loves you always, right through eternity. Rabi'a al-'Adawiyya (c. 717–801), the Sufi Muslim, wrote of finding this mature knowledge of God's love within herself, "I love God: I have no time left in which to hate the devil."[18]

A Prayer to Get Started

God of this life and the next, thank you for your mercy and love, now and always. Thank you for the promise of eternal life. Thank you for the ways in which those who have died continue to enrich our lives. Help us find gifts in our grief so that we may meet bereavement with peace and strength. Help us live well so that we can meet death well. Help us learn that death is not to be feared, but, in your timing, to be embraced. In the name of you, whom Mechthild of Magdeburg said draws the soul like a needle to a magnet upon death, Amen.

Questions for Journaling and Reflection

1. What does nature teach you about death? How does it make you feel when leaves begin to drop from the trees in the fall? When you see the first crocus of the spring? Is your grief soothed by the cycle of nature, or enraged by it, or untouched by it? Or perhaps you have a different reaction completely.

2. Allow your grief to encompass ritual. It may be as simple as planting an iris bulb each fall because it was your sister's favorite flower. Or you may find comfort in praying the Daily Office, prayers offered throughout the day by Christians all over the world. You can find these in prayer books like the Episcopal Book of Common Prayer. Some people find great comfort in writing letters to those whom they've lost on anniversaries they shared.

3. Several years ago, I ran across the following quote from the German theologian Dietrich Bonhoeffer (1906–1945), who was put to death by the Nazis for his role in the Christian resistance movement. Bonhoeffer wrote,

> *Nothing can make up for the absence of someone whom we love, and it would be wrong to try to find a substitute; we must simply hold out and see it through. That sounds very hard at first, but at the same time it is a great consolation, for the gap, as long as it remains unfilled, preserves the bonds between us. It is nonsense to say that God fills the gap; He doesn't fill it, but on the contrary, he keeps it empty and so helps us to keep alive our former communion with each other, even at the cost of pain.*[19]

Do you think Bonhoeffer is right, that God allows the gap between our dead loved ones and ourselves to exist? Have you experienced such a gap in your own grieving? If so, what has that gap meant in your relationship with those who have died? With God?

4. Allow yourself to think about how you'd like to be remembered. From my experience as a parish priest, I can tell you that one of the greatest gifts you can leave your family is to plan your funeral. It's a chore few people enjoy, but the peace of mind it will give you is worth the time. Write a brief description of your funeral—give your imagination and creativity free reign! And plan one ASAP.

5. Think about the solace you've received when you've lost loved ones. I describe my own journey toward solace after my young husband's death was labored, surprising, difficult, and slow. How would you describe your journey to solace?

13

NEW BEGINNINGS

My friend Carol, a few years ahead of me and decades wiser, defined middle age in a new way for me the other day: "Middle age is all about finding the other hand," she claims. "Middle age is full of new beginnings, but on the other hand, most of the time we don't want to begin, so you have to get good at finding the other hand. For instance, everybody dreads menopause, and it's *not* fun, but on the other hand, you never have to worry about birth control again. So menopause may be a pain, but it's also a new beginning. And most days, most of us dislike our children needing us less, but on the other hand, there's some relief and satisfaction, and a lot more time for yourself when you have an empty nest. And grandchildren give you a whole new reason to live. Middle age is just about finding the beginnings with the endings."

Carol should know. Divorced when her children were young, she's recently retired after years as a librarian, and now, while working in a bookstore to help supplement her income, she's writing a novel—a gutsy new beginning she's chosen for herself. Carol didn't exactly choose to retire; it was foisted upon her via downsizing. "But the timing is good," she insists optimistically, citing a survey that says you're most likely to write a blockbuster novel that tops the *New York Times* Bestseller List the year you turn fifty.[1]

Our mystics give us example after example of spending the second half of life fruitfully—in some cases, more fruitfully than the first half. Consider Teresa of Avila, who believed she wasted her youth. Her visionary experiences began at age forty and informed the twenty-seven remaining years of her life, which she spent reforming the Carmelites by traipsing across Spain founding convents and writing spiritual directions to her followers. In her early forties, Angela of Foligno lost her husband, sons, and mother within the space of a year, a grief with which she eventually coped by serving as the spiritual mother to the Franciscans for the rest of her life. Hildegard of Bingen's illness at age forty-two ended when "Heaven was opened" and she began writing her visions, and in general growing into herself. She founded two convents: one at age fifty-seven, and a second at age sixty-seven. At age seventy-two, Hildegard embarked on her fourth preaching tour in what is now Germany. Julian of Norwich's near-death experience that determined her life and ministry came at age thirty, and she wrote the Long Text of her *Revelations of Divine Love* in her fifties. Mechthild of Magdeburg was in her forties when she began her life work, *The Flowing Light of the Godhead*; she was blind, and in her sixties when she moved into a sort of assisted living situation at the convent at Helfta, still at work on *Flowing Light*.

But our mystics weren't women who sailed through life. Teresa of Avila was able to write about spiritual dryness because she had endured it, and was its reluctant student. Yet she was also able to write of triumph about the woman I suspect at least a part of each of us longs to become:

Her heart is full of joy with love,
For in the Lord her mind is stilled.
She has renounced every selfish attachment
And draws abiding joy and strength from the One within.
She lives not for herself, but lives
To serve the Lord of Love in all,
And swims across the sea of life
Breasting its rough waters joyfully[2]

Perhaps Teresa was able to write about drawing strength from the divine, and the deep joy it brings because she knew what it was like to live fearfully. The sea of life, Teresa knew, is full of rough waters. When the time came that Teresa felt God was calling her to leave the convent that had been her home for over-half her life, she procrastinated because "the cell in which I lived was just what I wanted." In fact, she reflected that she had actually entered the convent in the first place out of fear—fear of hell, fear of who she really was, fear of the world at large—certainly not out of love of God. In her autobiography, Teresa wrote sympathetically and realistically "that many who desire to withdraw from the world . . . and flee worldly dangers, find themselves in ten worlds joined together without knowing how to protect themselves or remedy the situation."[3] Teresa's sensitivity indicates that she was able to forgive herself for the fear she was also able to overcome. And her story assures that overcoming the fear many of us feel as we shift into mid- and late life is a common experience—not an easy experience, but a common one.

Julian of Norwich, who writes so convincingly that "all shall be well," also writes at length about fear, having learned about four kinds of fear in her visions. The first is "fear of assault, which comes . . . suddenly through timidity." Julian sees this as a natural fear—in our day, we would probably call this kind of fear a self-protective reflex—and reminds us that living through fearful situations helps to "purge" us by putting fear in perspective. One summer when I was consumed by orchestrating a complicated move to another state, I was afraid of things like the wrong belongings getting to the destination and the painter's schedule colliding with the tag sale. And then my son became seriously ill—which put my fear in perspective.

Julian writes that the second kind of fear is fear of pain, by which she means the pain of growth. She's not talking about being afraid that your knees will go if you begin walking every day, she's talking about the fear of living a more disciplined life. It isn't easy, Julian says, but when we step into our fear of change we become "able to receive the gentle strength of the Holy Spirit"—which will sustain us as we make transitions and changes. I'm heartened that the divine strength is described as "gentle," because for me, courage tends to come in fits and starts, and so the idea of the Holy Spirit as gentle and patient encourages me to be the same with myself.

The third fear, Julian writes, is "a doubtful fear; if it be recognized for what it is, however little it may be, it is a kind of despair." Anxiety is how I term what Julian calls "doubtful fear." When every decision—from how to respond to a grown child's choice of partner to pulling together a simple dinner—churns your stomach, that's doubtful fear. You're consumed by doubt, doubting your own competence, doubting the loyalty of those you love, doubting the love of God. Julian comments, "I am certain that God hates all doubtful fear, and he wishes us to drive it out, knowing how truly we may live." We are created to live in confidence and joy, and meant to enjoy our lives, not squander them on worry. When I start to regret how much of my life I've spent worrying, it helps to recall Julian's reminder that even God wants me to live without anxiety, and so I can be strengthened and glad knowing God is pleased for me.

The fourth kind of fear, Julian explains, is "reverent fear,

[and] there is no fear in us which pleases him but reverent fear. . . . And yet this reverent fear is not the same as love."⁴ So while God appreciates our attempts to love through fear—fear of being called a bad person, for instance—it is love for the sake of loving that we are to aim for. If you're feeling confused about the direction you want to take your life, this goal of loving for the sake of love can give you clarity and meaning.

I should have learned this lesson many years ago when I was kid learning how to garden at a place called "Hilltop." A couple mornings a week through the spring and summer, my friend Sue and I joined scores of other local kids to plant and weed our little plot. Midway through the morning, we broke for a meeting with the head of the program, white-headed Dr. Shulucha, who vehemently hated concrete ("stifles the soul") as much as much as she ardently loved dirt. As she enthusiastically enacted the importance of earthworms and led us in rousing choruses of "Hilltop's the Place for Me!," the grad students who worked for her would place a small golden-painted (well, golden spray paint) pot upside down on the stakes of particularly well-tended plots. Sue and I had countless squabbles about why we weren't receiving any golden pots, and one morning, a couple of grad students commented, "If you girls spent as much time weeding and watering as you do arguing about the golden pot, you might actually see one on your stake." Well!

That sharply true piece of advice was delivered decades ago, but only recently have I come to think of seeking opportunities for the sake of looking important to others as chasing the golden pot. And besides, there's a satisfaction that tending the vegetables gives you that golden pots are powerless to bestow. Maybe I should have learned the "lesson of the golden pot" when I was in grade school. But I didn't. I'm learning it now, and learning to be grateful for learning the lesson at all instead of blaming myself for not learning it earlier.

Thankfully, Jesus is much more concerned with who we are becoming than with who we were, telling Margery, "I take no heed what a man has been, but I take heed of what he will be." It's reassuring that even Margery herself dug in her heels when Jesus led her to new beginnings. When she was sixty-something, Margery whined when Jesus asked her to accompany her recently widowed daughter-in-law and grandchild to Germany, claiming she didn't have enough money, and that her unappreciative daughter-in-law was unwilling to help her. Jesus promised, "I shall provide for thee, and get thee friends to help thee. Do as I bid thee, and no man of the ship shall say nay to thee."[5] And so it was.

Likewise, sixty-eight-year-old Birgitta pled illness and infirmity when Jesus insisted she visit the Holy Land. His response? "I will be with you and I will direct your road, and I will lead you thither and lead you back to Rome, and I will provide you more amply with what you need than ever before."[6] And so He did.

Both Margery and Birgitta lived not only to tell the tale of their journeys, but to be enriched by the experiences. Besides, feeling your God-given empowerment can make you feel gloriously young. Hildegard wrote, "Sometimes—but not often—I see within this light another light, which I call 'the living Light.' And I cannot describe when and how I see it, but while I see it all sorrow and anguish leave me, so that then I feel like a simple girl instead of an old woman."[7]

There is no need for fear. Although she knew fear, Julian herself had to learn that she need not experience it. In the last chapter of her Long Text, she writes, "So I was taught that love is our Lord's meaning. And I saw very certainly in this and in everything that before God made us he loved us, which love has never abated and never will be. And in this love he has done all his works, and in this love he has made all things profitable to us, and in this love our life is everlasting. In our creation we had our beginning, but the love in which he created us was in him from without beginning. In this love we have our beginning, and in all this shall we see in God without end."[8]

Our mystics are always leading us back to love. It is love that made us, love that sustains us, and love that it is ours for all eternity. "Love me with all your heart," Jesus tells Margery, "for I love you with all mine. My merciful eyes are ever upon you."[9] A simple truth, but hard to remember.

Mechthild of Magdeburg wrote a particularly moving poem describing God's eternal longing for us. She so beautifully describes God's audacious yearning for our love that I don't have the heart to omit a word of it.

> *God Speaks to the soul: And God said to the soul: I desired you before the world began. I desire you now As you desire me. And where the desires of two come together There love is perfected.*
> *How the Soul Speaks to the Soul: Lord, you are my lover, My longing, My flowing stream, My sun, And I am your reflection.*
>
> *How God Answers The Soul: It is my nature that makes me love you often, For I am love itself. It is my longing that makes me love you intensely, For I yearn to be loved from the heart. It is my eternity that makes me love you long, For I have no end.*[10]

So don't hold back on asking God for help! God is talking to *the* soul, *your* soul. God is love, and wants only for us to reflect that love back as best we can. Evidently, part of being God is longing for *you*—and longing to help you. Remember this promise from Isaiah? "Those who wait for the LORD shall renew their strength, they shall mount up with wings like eagles,

they shall run and not be weary, they shall walk and not faint"
(Isaiah 40:31).

We grow up learning it's dangerous to discuss politics or
religion; the medieval world was suffused with religion, which,
by the way, encompassed politics. While we may disagree with
the medieval world view, we can borrow the conviction that God
is an always available, always enthusiastic source of renewal,
longing to meet us heart to heart.

Catherine of Siena adopts a "just do it" attitude: "Start being
brave about everything. Drive out darkness and spread light.
Don't look at your weaknesses. Realize instead that in Christ
crucified you can do everything."[11] You can imagine Catherine
adopting this advice as her mantra on her way to confront Pope
Gregory XI. After leading twenty-three people a distance of
roughly five hundred miles, from what is now northern Italy to
the south of France, she stood at the foot of the formidable
Palace of the Popes—where she probably felt as unsure of herself
as Dorothy at the gate of the Emerald City. Yet, when a friend
of hers was intimidated by undertaking a similar journey and
meeting, Catherine was able to cheerlead, "No more indifference
then! No more sleeping in unawareness! No, with bold and blazing heart stretch your sweet loving desires to go and give honor
to God and your best efforts to your neighbors, never losing sight
of your objective."

I love Catherine's phrase "bold and blazing heart" because it
speaks to me of the surge of certainty so many of us middle-aged
women feel, even if we may be uncertain about how to express it.
I think the key to unlocking the "bold and blazing" parts of our
hearts sometimes lies in the hands of others. We need not think
we're ever too old to need help. No matter how "independent" we
may have been, or are, we can be more of who we are through
healthy friendships.

In Catherine of Genoa's "Indian Summer," she found a new

beginning in the last decade of her life. Catherine had always navigated her spiritual struggles completely on her own. But at age fifty-three, Catherine found a spiritual director who thought of himself as more her student than her teacher. With the help of Father Don Cattaneo Marabotto, she found a new peace in her spirituality—and was able to write her autobiography, which Christians have found helpful for the past five hundred years.

Like Catherine of Genoa, and like all our mystics for that matter, Margery also found her spiritual path full of potholes. She once described herself as uncertain, as a reed stalk blowing with the wind. And I think she was lonely. All her attempts to be herself (or at least who she *thought* herself was at that point), her forays into business, her pilgrimages, her worship, everything she did seemed to drive people away from her. She writes of scant friendships, but she ends her autobiography praying for others. And in this maturity, Margery finally found peace.

It takes courage to grow and change, no matter what our age, and sometimes I think Margery, like so many of us, was able to grow into praying for others only because she was so miserable being self-centered. Part of the reason it's hard to move into the future God has in mind for us is because we're unable to see it. As Paul reminds us in 1 Corinthians 12, in this life, we see in a mirror, dimly, but in the in next life, we shall see God face to face. We'll no longer know in part, but shall know fully, even as we have been fully known. So we stumble on in this life, with grace surrounding us.

When I was a young bride, my husband and I both found jobs in Pittsburgh, which turned out to be a wonderful place (to this day, it's my favorite city), with plentiful friends and interesting jobs for both of us. It was also a marvelous place for our son, who would be born more than three years later, to have his beginning. Of course I didn't know that's how Pittsburgh— where we'd both found jobs—would turn out as we prepared to move from my hometown, where we'd met while graduate students. I came down with what a therapist told me was "severe separation anxiety." It helped to untangle some of this with her, but I think it was a cleaning lady who worked in my office who helped me the most. "When I was young like you, I moved from my hometown. It was hard, but ever since, I've been able to move anywhere. It's a gift, being able to live anywhere, you know," she told me over her mops and brooms, "but you won't find that gift as long as you stay here."

I wish I could remember the cleaning lady's name, but I've never forgotten her words. They carried me into a more expansive life nestled in Pittsburgh's beautiful river-run hills. After my husband's death, it was time to move our son and myself into a still-more expansive life at Yale, where new friends, new ideas and healing awaited. New Haven lived up to its name. It was there that I first met many of the mystics in this book. It's been time to move on since, but always God carries me, and always I carry friendships, some of them quite mystical.

Now is the time for you to become friends with the mystics. Their wisdom awaits you.

A PRAYER TO GET STARTED

God of all beginnings, of the beginning of water, air, fire, and of each of our beginnings and endings: Thank you. Thank you for the mystics, who are there to guide us through the waves, the wind, the flames, of our lives. Thank you for Teresa's humor, for Margery's honesty, for Julian's openness, for Catherine's courage, for Clare's conviction. Thank you for the wisdom and friendship of them all. In the name of You, who creates each of us with gifts to share, Amen.

Questions for Journaling and Reflection

1. Of all the mystics we've met, which one do you connect with most naturally? Julian, Teresa, Hildegard, one of the Catherines, or Mechthilds or Margurites, Margery, Angela, Birgitta, Clare, Elisabeth, Gertrude? Why? And who leaves you cold? What are they trying to teach you?

2. I've shared with you how hard it was for me to move to Pittsburgh, a place I came to love, so that when it came time to leave, that was difficult too. Think back on some of the most difficult changes you've had to make. How have they shaped who you are today? What can your younger self tell your current self to guide you through upcoming changes?

3. How do you begin and end each day? Find a way to focus yourself on God—something as simple and informal as a quick prayer of "thank you," or something as elaborate and disciplined as saying the rosary—at the beginning and the end of the day for a month, and notice any changes it makes.

4. I hope this book will be the beginning of an enriched spiritual life for you. Perhaps it will also be the beginning of an online community. In any case, here's my e-mail: wisdom4midlife@gmail.com.

NOTES

INTRODUCTION

1.   Ursula King, *Christian Mystics: Their Lives and Legacies through-out the Ages* (Mahwah, NJ: HiddenSpring, 2001), 3.

2.   Catherine of Genoa, quoted in Ursula King, *Christian Mystics: The Spiritual Heart of the Christian Tradition* (New York: Simon & Schuster, 1998), 90.

3.   Carol Lee Flinders, *Enduring Grace: Living Portraits of Seven Women Mystics* (New York: HarperCollins, 1993), 103.

4.   *Revelations of Divine Love* by Julian of Norwich

5.   Mark Atherton, trans., *Hildegard of Bingen: Selected Writings* (London: Penguin Classics, 2001), xx.

6.   Flinders, *Enduring Grace*, 11.

7.   Ibid., 112.

8.   Dylan Thomas wrote "The Force That Through the Green Fuse Drives the Flower" around 1932, when he was eighteen.

9.   Catherine of Genoa, quoted in Carol Lee Flinders, *A Little Book of Women Mystics* (HarperSanFrancisco, 1995), 76.

10.   Catherine of Siena, quoted in Flinders, *Enduring Grace*

CHAPTER 1

1. For updated interpretations of Genesis 2–3, see, for instance, Elaine Pagels, *Adam, Eve, and the Serpent* (London: Weidenfeld & Nicholson, 1988); or Barbara Grizzati Harrison's essay, "A Meditation on Eve," in *Out of the Garden: Women Writers on the Bible* (New York: Ballantine, 1995).

2. According to a National Vital Statistics Report of November 10, 2004, American women's life expectancy is now pushing eighty. Medievalists don't have enough evidence to report with certainty what life expectancy was back then, but what with deaths caused by childbirth, war, famine, the plague, and other diseases, it was certainly significantly shorter than ours—usually estimated at thirty in plague times, around forty in non-plague times. Of course, these numbers take into account the high infant and child mortality rate.

3. Carol Lee Flinders, ed., *A Little Book of Women Mystics* (San Francisco: HarperSanFrancisco, 1995), 9–10.

4. Ibid., 10.

5. Angela of Foligno, *Memoriale*, chap. 6, quoted in "Other Women's Voices," http://home.infionline.net/~ddisse/angela. html.

6. "Other Women's Voices," http://home.infionline.net.

7. Clare of Assisi, quoted in, "Other Women's Voices," http://home.infionline.net/~ddisse/ clare.html.

8. Agatha Christie, *An Autobiography* (New York: Dodd, Mead and Company, 1977).

9. From the Long Text, chap. 37, in Monica Furlong, ed., *The Wisdom of Julian of Norwich* (Oxford: Lion Publishing PLC, 1996), 41.

10. Teresa of Avila, quoted in, Carol Lee Flinders, ed., *A Little Book of Women Mystics* (HarperSanFrancisco, 1995), 98.

11. Carol Lee Flinders, *Enduring Grace: Living Portraits of Seven Women Mystics* (New York: HarperCollins, 1993), 111.

12. As quoted by Cecelia Goodnow, "Women Turn Midlife on Its Head," *Seattle Post-Intelligencer*, April 25, 2005.

13. As quoted by Heather Salerno, "Women in the Middle," *Journal News* (Westchester, Rockland, and Putnam Counties, New York), May 1, 2005.

CHAPTER 2

1. Joan Hamilton, "Woman of the Year," *Town & Country*, January 2006.

2. Ski Hunter, Sandra S. Sundel, and Martin Sundel, *Women at Midlife: Life Experience and Implications for the Helping Professions* (Washington, DC: National Association of Social Workers, 2002).

3. Carol Lee Flinders, *Enduring Grace: Living Portraits of Seven Women Mystics* (New York: HarperCollins, 1993), 11.

4. Carol Lee Flinders ed., *A Little Book of Women Mystics* (HarperSanFrancisco, 1995), 58–59.

5. As noted in a poetic presentation given by Professor Talat Halman (Turkey's first cultural minister) and actress Defne Halman, February 23, 2005, Stevens Institute of Technology, Hoboken, NJ.

6. Monica Furlong, *Visions and Longings: Medieval Women Mystics* (Boston: Shambhala, 1997), 14.

7. Flinders, *Enduring Grace*, 78.

8. Extracts from *The Liber Celestis* by Birgitta of Sweden in Elizabeth Spearing, ed., *Medieval Writings on Female Spirituality* (New York, Penguin Books, 2002), 160.

9. Dorothy Disse, ed., "Other Women's Voices," http://home.infionline.net/~ddisse/julian.html.

10. Julian of Norwich, Revelations of Divine Love, trans. Clifton Wolters (London: Penguin Classics, 1966), chap. 56 of the Long Text, 161.

11. Julia Bolton Holloway, "The Cell of Self-Knowledge: The Soul Within," http://www.umilta.net/cell.html.

12. Julian of Norwich, Revelations of Divine Love, chap. 5 of the Long Text, 67–68.

13. Ibid., 68.

14. Fred Rogers, "Life's Journeys according to Mister Rogers" calendar, February 25/26, 2006. Used by permission

15. Julian of Norwich, Revelations of Divine Love, chap. 14 of the Long Text, 85.

16. Edmund Colledge and James Walsh, eds., *Julian of Norwich: Showings* (New York: Paulist Press, 1978), 255 and 258, quoted in Flinders, *A Little Book of Women Mystics*, 46–47.

CHAPTER 3

1. Ski Hunter, Sandra S. Sundel, and Martin Sundel, *Women at Midlife: Life Experience and Implications for the Helping Professions* (Washington, DC: National Association of Social Workers, 2002).

2. Christiane Northrup, *The Wisdom of Menopause: Creating Physical and Emotional Health and Healing During the Change* (New York: Bantam, 2001), 2.

3. Ibid.

4. Hildegard of Bingen, *Holistic Healing*, ed. and trans. Manfred Pawlik, Patrick Madigan, Mary Palmquist, and John Kulas (Collegeville, MN: Liturgical Press, 1994), 147.

5. Wighard Strehlow, *Hildegard of Bingen's Spiritual Remedies* (Rochester, VT: Healing Arts Press, 2002), introduction.

6. Catherine of Siena, quoted in, Carol Lee Flinders, *Enduring Grace: Living Portraits of Seven Women Mystics* (New York: HarperCollins, 1993), 110.

7. Extracts from *The Liber Celestis* by Birgitta of Sweden in Elizabeth Spearing, ed., *Medieval Writings on Female Spirituality* (New York, Penguin, 2002), 146.

8. Lynn Staley, ed. and trans., *The Book of Margery Kempe* (New York: Norton, 2001), 16.

9. Ibid., 101.

10. Ibid., 77.

11. Ibid., 57.

12. Ibid., 103.

13. "Other Women's Voices," http://home.infionline.net/~ddisse/mechthil.html.

14. Monica Furlong, *Visions and Longings: Medieval Women Mystics* (Boston: Shambhala, 1997), 29.

15. To learn more about the complex issues that shed light on why so many spiritually inclined medieval women indulged in anorexia and other forms of self-punishment, see Caroline Walker Bynum, *Holy Feast and Holy Fast: The Religious Significance of Food to Medieval Women* (Berkeley: University of California Press, 1987); and Elizabeth A. Petroff, *Body and Soul: Essays on Medieval Women and Mysticism* (New York: Oxford University Press, 1995).

16. Hildegard of Bingen, *The Book of the Rewards of Life*, trans. Bruce W. Hozeski (New York: Oxford University Press, 1977), 74.

17. Ibid., 89.

CHAPTER 4

1. Eileen Power, *Medieval Women* (Cambridge: Cambridge University Press, 1995), 85.

2. Frank Tobin, *Mechthild of Magdeburg: The Flowing Light of the Godhead* (New York: Paulist Press, 1998), 52.

3. Ibid., 193.

4. Ibid., 31.

5. Abby Stoner, "Gender and the Medieval Beguines," http://user-www.sfsu.edu/~epf/1995/beguine.html.

6. Marianne Dorman, "The Beguines," http://mariannedorman. homestead.com.Beguines.html.

7. On the other hand, Mechthild of Hackeborn could have been Dante's model, or perhaps he used both. Thanks to Yale's Peter S. Hawkins for his expertise.

6. Marianne Dorman, "The Beguines," http://mariannedorman. homestead.com.Beguines.html.

8. Tobin, *Mechthild of Magdeburg*, 96–97.

9. Ibid.

10. Sue Ellen Cooper, *The Red Hat Society: Fun and Friendship after Fifty* (New York: Warner Books, 2004), 70.

11. Cynthia Hubert, "Best Friends: When It Comes to Relationships, There's No Match for the Bond Between Women," *Sacramento Bee*, March 5, 2006, L1.

CHAPTER 5

1. Barbara Cawthorne Crafton, "Rematch: The Old Enemies," The Almost Daily eMo, June 7, 2004, http://www.geraniumfarm.org/daily emo.cfm?Emo=274.

2. I recount this story in the introduction to *Prayers to the God of My Life: Psalms for Morning and Evening* (Harrisburg, PA: Morehouse Publishing, 2001).

3. *New York Times*, Women's Health Special Edition, June 21, 1998,

http://www.nytimes.com/specials/women/ whome/depression.html.

4. "Other Women's Voices," http://home.infionline.net/~ddisse/teresa.html.

5. Lynn Staley, ed. and trans., *The Book of Margery Kempe* (New York: Norton, 2001), 7.

6. Ibid.

7. "Other Women's Voices." You can listen to the Taizé chant based on Teresa's poem at http://www.taize.fr/ext/sound/mp3/nadate.mp3. The chant is also recorded on the CD *Laudate Omnes Gentes*.

8. Daniel Ko, "Religious Coping Plays a Role in Recovery from Depression," http://www.mental-health-today.com/articles/spirituality.htm.

9. Julian of Norwich, *Revelations of Divine Love*, chap. 22 of the Short Text, in *The Wisdom of Julian of Norwich*, ed. Monica Furlong (Grand Rapids, MI: Eerdmans, 1996), 18.

10. Ibid., 47.

11. Ibid., 31

12. Ibid., 21.

13. Elisabeth of Schonau, quoted in, "Other Women's Voices," http://home.infionline.net/~ddisse /schonau.html.

14. Elisabeth of Schonau, *Visions—Book Two*, trans. Thalia A. Pandiri, in *Medieval Women's Visionary Literature* (New York: Oxford University Press, 1986), 165.

15. The Virgin Mary answered that she was fifteen. Ibid., 170.

16. Evelyn Underhill, *Mysticism* (1911), "Voices and Visions," http://www.ccel.org/ccel/underhill/mysticism.html, 270.

17. Julian of Norwich, *Revelations of Divine Love*, trans. Clifton Wolters (London: Penguin Classics, 1966), chap. 13 of the Long Text, 84.

18. Barbara Cawthorne Crafton, "Rematch: The Old Enemies," The Almost Daily eMo, June 7, 2004, http://www.geraniumfarm.org/dailyemo.cfm?Emo=274

CHAPTER 6

1. Catherine of Siena, quoted in, Carol Lee Flinders, ed., *A Little Book of Women Mystics* (HarperSanFrancisco, 1995), 63.

2. Catherine of Siena, quoted in, Carol Lee Flinders, *Enduring*

Grace: Living Portraits of Seven Women Mystics (New York: HarperCollins, 1993), 104.

3. Ibid., 112.

4. Wim van den Dungen, trans., *On Seven Ways of Holy Love by Beatrice of Nazareth*, http://www.sofiatopia.org.equiaeon/7ways.htm.

5. Julian of Norwich, *Revelations of Divine Love*, chap. 27 of the Long Text, in *The Wisdom of Julian of Norwich*, ed. Monica Furlong (Grand Rapids: Eerdmans, 1996), 41.

6. Julian of Norwich, *Revelations of Divine Love*, trans. Clifton Wolters (London: Penguin Classics, 1966), chap. 13 of the Long Text, 84.

7. Ursula King, *Christian Mystics: Their Lives and Legacies throughout the Ages* (Mahwah, NJ: HiddenSpring, 2001), 87.

8. Dante Alighieri, *Inferno*, trans. Martin Robertson, http://rtnl.org.uk/now_and_then/html/151.html, canto 7, vv. 121–24.

9. Julian of Norwich, *Revelations of Divine Love*, chap. 15 of the Long Text, in Furlong, ed., *The Wisdom of Julian of Norwich*, 28.

10. From chap. 50 of the Long Text of Julian's *Revelations of Divine Love*, modernized by Sheila Upjohn in *Why Julian Now? A Voyage of Discovery* (Grand Rapids, MI: Eerdmans, 1997), 22–23.

11. Frances and Joseph Gies, *Women in the Middle Ages* (New York: HarperPerennial, 1978), 64.

12. Gertrude of Helfta, *The Herald II*, quoted in Jane Klimisch, "Gertrude of Helfta: A Woman God-Filled and Free," in *Medieval Women Monastics: Wisdom's Wellsprings*, ed. Miriam Schmitt and Linda Kulzer (Collegeville, MN: Liturgical Press, 1996), 252.

13. Ibid., 253.

14. Teresa Wolking, "Hrotsvit: Medieval Playwright," in *Medieval Women Monastics*, 137–47. See also "Other Women's Voices," http://home.infionline.net/~ddisse/hrotsvit.html.

15. Eliabeth Alvida Petroff, "Women, Heresy, and Holiness in Early Fourteenth-Century France," *Medieval Women's Visionary Literature* (New York: Oxford University Press, 1986), 282.

16. Ibid.

17. Victoria R. Sirota, June 23, 1997; revised June 7, 2006, for this book.

CHAPTER 7

1. Carol Lee Flinders, ed., *A Little Book of Women Mystics* (HarperSanFrancisco, 1995), 4.

2. Interview, *Religion and Ethics Newsweekly*, PBS, April 11, 2003. Among Zaleski's books on spirituality is *Prayer: A History*, written with Carol Zaleski (Boston: Houghton Mifflin, 2002).

3. Teresa of Avila, *Interior Castle*, chap. 2.2, in *The Collected Works of St. Teresa of Avila*, vol. 2, trans. Kieran Kavanaugh and Otilio Rodriguez (Washington, DC: Institute of Carmelite Studies, 1980).

4. Elizabeth Dreyer, "Passionate Women: Two Medieval Mystics," Madeleva Lecture in Spirituality (New York: Paulist Press, 1989), 21.

5. Richard Rolle, *The Fire of Love*, http://people.bu.edu/dklepper/RN413/rolle.html.

6. Sheila Upjohn, *Why Julian Now? A Voyage of Discovery* (Grand Rapids, MI: Eerdmans, 1997), 122–30.

7. From chap. 43 of the Long Text of Julian of Norwich, *Revelations of Divine Love*, modernized by Sheila Upjohn in *Why Julian Now? A Voyage of Discovery*, 123.

8. John Kirvan, *Let Nothing Disturb You: A Journey to the Center of the Soul with Teresa of Avila* (Notre Dame, IN: Ave Maria Press, 2001), 11.

9. "Images of Violence in the Medieval World," December 21, 2004–March 13, 2005.

10. Regis J. Armstrong, ed. and trans., *Clare of Assisi: Early Documents* (New York: Paulist Press, 1988), 44, quoted in Carol Lee Flinders, *Enduring Grace: Living Portraits of Seven Women Mystics* (New York: HarperCollins, 1993), 23.

11. Ibid., 24.

12. From chap. 31 of the Long Text in *The Wisdom of Julian of Norwich*, ed. Monica Furlong (Grand Rapids: Eerdmans, 1996), 36.

13. Teresa of Avila, *Interior Castle*, chap. 2.2.

14. For more on medieval contemplative prayer, see *The Cloud of Unknowing*, the anonymous classic from fourteenth-century England that stresses the importance of intuition over reason in prayer. For a more modern take on contemplative prayer, see the work of Thomas Merton (1915–1968).

15. "Other Women's Voices," http://home.infionlin.net/~ddisse/mechthil.html.

16. "Other Women's Voices," http://home.infionlin.net/~ddisse/teresa.html.

CHAPTER 8

1. Catherine of Siena, *Catherine of Siena: The Dialogue*, trans. Suzanne Noffke (New York: Paulist Press, 1980), quoted in Carol Lee Flinders, ed., *A Little Book of Women Mystics* (San Francisco: HarperSan Francisco, 1995), 66.

2. Judith Viorst, *Grown-Up Marriage: What We Know, Wish We Had Known, and Still Need to Know about Being Married* (New York: Free Press, 2004), excerpt from simonsays.com.

3. Correspondence with author, April 2007.

4. Thomas Cahill, *Mysteries of the Middle Ages: The Rise of Feminism, Science, and Art from the Cults of Catholic Europe* (New York: Doubleday, 2006), 121.

5. U.S. Department of Justice, Violence by Intimates: Analysis of Data on Crimes by Current or Former Spouses, Boyfriends, and Girlfriends, March 1998. www.endabuse.org/resources/fact.

6. Commonwealth Fund, Health Concerns across a Woman's Lifespan: 1998 Survey of Women's Health, May 1999. www.endabuse.org/resources/fact.

7. Frances and Joseph Gies, *Women in the Middle Ages* (New York: HarperPerennial, 1978), 46–47. And, if you were waiting for the example of "the rule of thumb" coming from old English law allowing husbands to beat their wives so long as the stick they used wasn't any wider than their thumbs, well, I assumed I'd include it as well. But it turns out that's just, pardon the expression, an old wives' tale.

8. Catherine of Genoa, *Life and Doctrine of Saint Catherine of Genoa*, trans. Mrs. George Ripley (New York: Christian Press Association Publishing, 1896), quoted in Flinders, *Enduring Grace*, 138.

9. Ibid., 132–33.

10. Christiane Northrup, *The Wisdom of Menopause: Creating Physical and Emotional Health and Healing During the Change* (New York: Bantam Books, 2001), 29.

11. In December 2003, *AARP The Magazine* polled 581 men and 566 women who divorced between the ages of 40 and 70 for a study called "The Divorce Experience: A Study of Divorce At Midlife and Beyond"; results were published in May 2004.

12. Northrup, *The Wisdom of Menopause*, 30–31.

13. Translation by Coleman Barks. See www.colemanbarks.com.

14. Jennifer Ward, *Women in Medieval Europe 1200–1500* (Edinburgh: Longman, 2002), 174.

15. Catherine of Genoa, *Purgation and Purgatory, The Spiritual Dialogue,* trans. Serge Hughes (New York: Paulist Press, 1979), 80, quoted in Flinders, *Enduring Grace.*

16. http://www.marlapaul.com.

CHAPTER 9

1. Quoted in, "Other Women's Voices," http://home.infionline. net/~ddisse/dhuoda.html.

2. Ibid.

3. Julian of Norwich, *Revelations of Divine Love,* trans. Clifton Wolters (London: Penguin Classics, 1966), chap. 61 of the Long Text, 172–73.

4. Reported by Trish Hall in "Moms and Daughters, Too Close for Comfort," *New York Times,* June 21, 1998.

5. Catherine of Siena, quoted in, Ursula King, *Christian Mystics* (New York, Simon & Schuster, 1998), 85.

6. Suzanne Noffke, trans., *Catherine of Siena: Letters (Paulist Press, 1988),* 84, quoted in Carol Lee Flinders, ed., *A Little Book of Women Mystics* (HarperSanFrancisco, 1995), 68–69.

7. Ski Hunter, Sandra S. Sundel, and Martin Sundel, *Women at Midlife: Life Experience and Implications for the Helping Professions* (Washington, DC: National Association of Social Workers, 2002).

8. Hail, Mary, full of grace, the Lord is with thee; blessed art thou among women and blessed is the fruit of thy womb, Jesus. Holy Mary, Mother of God, pray for us sinners now and at the hour of our death.

9. Henry Adams, quoted in Thomas Cahill, *Mysteries of the Middle Ages: The Rise of Feminism, Science, and Art from the Cults of Catholic Europe* (New York: Doubleday, 2006), 109.

10. Cahill, *Mysteries of the Middle Ages*, 119.

11. Ibid., 108.

12. Quoted by Clarissa W. Atkinson, "Female Sanctity in the Late Middle Ages," in *The Book of Margery Kempe*, ed. and trans. Lynn Staley (New York: Norton, 2001), 232.

13. Julian of Norwich, *Revelations of Divine Love*, chap. 60 of the Long Text, 169.

14. Teresa of Avila, *The Way of Perfection*, trans. Kieran Kavanaugh and Otilio Rodriguez, chap. 31, 9, in *The Collected Works of St. Teresa of Avila*, vol. 2 (Washington, DC: Institute Carmelite Studies, 1980).

15. Marguerite d'Oingt, *Letters*, para. 137–38, quoted in Elizabeth Alvilda Petroff, *Medieval Women's Visionary Literature* (New York: Oxford University Press, 1986), 278.

16. Caroline Walker Bynum, *Jesus as Mother* (Los Angeles: University of California Press, 1982), 153.

17. "Other Women's Voices," http://home.infionline.net/~ddisse/dhuoda.html.

18. This story is found throughout literature on Clare; my sources include Eliabeth Alvida Petroff, "Women and Spirituality in Medieval Italy," *Medieval Women's Visionary Literature* (New York: Oxford University Press, 1986), 232 ff.

19. Julian of Norwich, *Revelations of Divine Love*, Clifton Wolters, trans. (London: Penguin Classics, 1966), Chapter 6 of Long Text, 70.

20. Ibid., 164.

21. Explored in-depth by Deborah Tannen in *You're Wearing That? Understanding Mothers and Daughters in Conversation* (New York: Random House, 2006).

22. *The Letters of Catherine of Siena*, translated with introduction and notes by Suzanne Noffke, Medieval & Renaissance Studies, 2000, volume 2, p.442, found on http://home.infionline.net/~ddisse/siena.html.

23. Hadewijch Letter 29, found on http://home.infionline.net/~ddisse/hadewijc.html.

24. "Other Women's Voices," http://home.infionlin.net/~ddisse/beatrijs.html.

CHAPTER 10

1.   Dhuoda of Septimania, quoted in, "Other Women's Voices," http://home.infionline.net/~ddisse/ dhuoda.html.

2.   Clare of Assisi, quoted in, "Other Women's Voices," http://home.infionline.net/~ddisse/ clare.html.

3.   Hildegard of Bingen, quoted in, "Other Women's Voices," http://home.infionline.net/~ddisse/ hildegar.html.

4.   Regis J. Armstrong, ed. and trans. *Clare of Assisi: Early Documents* (New York: Paulist Press, 1988), 47, quoted in Carol Lee Flinders, *Enduring Grace: Living Portraits of Seven Women Mystics* (New York: HarperCollins, 1993), 16–17.

5.   Clare of Assisi, quoted in, "Other Women's Voices," http://home.infionline.net/~ddisse/ clare.html.

6.   Norman P. Tanner, *The Church in Late Medieval Norwich 1370–1532*, Studies and Texts 66 (Toronto: Pontifical Institute of Mediaeval Studies, 1984), 159.

7.   Lynn Staley, ed. and trans., *The Book of Margery Kempe* (New York: Norton, 2001), 6.

8.   Frances and Joseph Gies, *Women in the Middle Ages* (New York: HarperPerennial, 1978), 183.

9.   Ibid., 147.

10.   Ibid., 178–79.

11.   Ibid., 182–83.

12.   Mother Columba Hart, ed. and trans., *Hadewijch: The Complete Works* (New York: Paulist Press, 1980), 5.

13.   "Other Women's Voices," http://home.infionline.net/~ddisse/ hadewijc.html.

14.   Hadewijch of Brabant, quoted in, "Other Women's Voices," http://home.infionline.net/~ddisse/hadewijc.html.

15.   Unless otherwise noted, quotations from Hadewijch are translated by Eric Colledge, and found in Eliabeth Alvida Petroff, *Medieval Women's Visionary Literature* (New York: Oxford University Press, 1986), 189-95.

16.   Ski Hunter, Sandra S. Sundel, and Martin Sundel, *Women at Midlife: Life Experience and Implications for the Helping Professions* (Washington, DC: National Association of Social Workers, 2002).

17. "Other Women's Voices," http://home.infionline.net/~ddisse/hadewijc.html.

CHAPTER 11

1. Teresa Wolking, "Hrotsvit: Medieval Playwright," in *Medieval Women Monastics: Wisdom's Wellsprings* (Collegeville, MN: Liturgical Press, 1996), 141.

2. Carol Lee Flinders, *Enduring Grace: Living Portraits of Seven Women Mystics* (New York: HarperCollins, 1993), 227.

3. "Other Women's Voices," http://home.infionline.net/ddisse/siena.html.

4. Reported by Barbara Beckwith in "St. Catherine of Siena: A Feisty Role for Sister Nancy Murray," *St. Anthony Messenger* online, April 2006.

5. *The English Text of the Ancrene Riwle* (London: Oxford University Press, 1972), 305.

6. Sarah Law, "'A Room of Her Own' Julian, Prayer and Creativity," 2003 Annual Julian Lecture, St. Julian's Church, Norwich, England, May 3, 2003, 5.

7. Grant S. Carey, "A Visit with Margery Kemp," Trinity Cathedral, Sacramento, California, www.trinitycathedral.org/about_carey_corner8.shtml.

8. Suzanne Noffke, trans., *Catherine of Siena: Letters* (Paulist Press, 1988), 45, quoted in Carol Lee Flinders, ed., *A Little Book of Women Mystics* (HarperSanFrancisco, 1995), 65–66.

9. Sarah Law, "A Room of Her Own," 7.

10. Barbara Cawthorne Crafton, "Jesus Claims Some Quiet Time," The Almost Daily eMo, February 1, 2006, http://www.geraniumfarm.org/dailyemo.cfm?Emo=604.

11. David Crawley, "The Green-Fingered God," *Reality Magazine* vol. 9, no. 52 (2002): 28.

12. Ibid., 29.

13. Deborah Vass, "The World Civilization Virtual Library," (Milledgeville: Georgia College & State University), http://www.faculty.de.gcsu.edu/~dvess/ids/fap/hildegard.htm.

14. Jennifer Ward, *Women in Medieval Europe 1200–1500*

(Edinburgh: Longman, 2002), 201.

15. Catherine of Siena, "Prayer 20," trans. Suzanne Noffke, www.poetry-chaikhana.com/C/CatherineofS/Wewereenclos.htm.

CHAPTER 12

1. *Liberty: Life in the Liberty Years, A Nostalgic Look at the '20's, '30's, and '40's* (Kansas City: Hallmark Cards, 1973), 44.

2. J. Paul Getty Museum, Los Angeles, CA, December 21, 2004–March 13, 2005.

3. Mark Atherton, trans., *Hildegard of Bingen: Selected Writings* (London: Penguin Classics, 2001), xvi.

4. Sometimes called the Song of Solomon, it is full of lusty imagery such as "You are stately as a palm tree, and your breasts are like its clusters. I say I will climb the palm tree and lay hold of its branches. O may your breasts be like clusters of the vine, and the scent of your breath like apples . . ." (7:7–8). Perhaps because of my Rubenesque figure, my favorite line is found at 7:1: "Your rounded thighs are like jewels."

5. Frances and Joseph Gies, *Women in the Middle Ages: The Lives of Real Women in a Vibrant Age of Transition* (New York: HarperPerennial, 1978), 81.

6. All quotes taken from translation of Beatrice's work by Wim van den Dungen, found at http://www.sofiatopia.org/equiaeon/7ways.htm.

7. Julian of Norwich, chap. 36 of the Long Text, in *Revelations of Divine Love*, in *The Wisdom of Julian of Norwich*, ed. Monica Furlong (Grand Rapids, MI: Eerdmans, 1996), 40.

8. Carol Lee Flinders, *Enduring Grace: Living Portraits of Seven Women Mystics* (HarperCollins, 1993), 116-17.

9. See http:/www.sofiatopia.org/equiaeon/7ways.htm.

10. Catherine of Genoa, quoted in, Carol Lee Flinders, ed., *A Little Book of Women Mystics* (Harper SanFrancisco, 1995), 81.

11. Ibid., 79.

12. Henri Nouwen, *The Inner Voice of Love* (New York: Doubleday, 1998), 64.

13. Elizabeth Alvida Petroff, "Women, Heresy, and Holiness in Early Fourteenth-Century France," in *Medieval Women's Visionary Literature* (New York: Oxford University Press, 1986), 282.

14. As quoted in Flinders, ed., *A Little Book of Women Mystics*, 62.

15. Hildegard of Bingen, quoted in, "Other Women's Voices" Http://home.infionline.net/~ddisse/ hildegar.html.

16. Fred Rogers, "Life's Journeys according to Mister Rogers" calendar, March 9, 2006. Used by permission.

17. Edmund Colledge and James Walsh, eds., *Julian of Norwich: Showings* (New York: Paulist Press, 1978), 255 and 258, quoted in Flinders, ed., *A Little Book of Women Mystics*, 46–47.

18. Rabi'a al-'Adawiyya, quoted in, "Other Women's Voices," http://home.infionlin.net/~ddisse/rabia.html.

19. Dietrich Bonhoeffer, *Letters and Papers from Prison*, ed. Eberhard Bethge (New York: Collier Books, 1972), 176.

Chapter 13

1. Study conducted by lulu.com. According to the study, released May 12, 2005, the average age of writers in the year that their novels topped the hardback fiction section of the *New York Times* Bestseller List from 1955–2004 was 50.5 years.

2. Teresa of Avila, translated by Eknath Easwaran in *God Makes the Rivers to Flow* (Petaluma, CA: Nilgiri Press, 1982), cited by Carol Lee Flinders, ed., in *A Little Book of Women Mystics* (New York: Harper SanFrancisco, 1995), 102–3.

3. Carol Lee Flinders, *Enduring Grace: Living Portraits of Seven Women Mystics* (New York: HarperCollins, 1993), 163.

4. Julian of Norwich, Short Text, *Revelations of Divine Love*, Chapter 25, as found in *The Wisdom of Julian of Norwich*, compiled and edited by Monica Furlong (Grand Rapids, MI: William B. Eerdmans Publishing Company, 1996), 234.

5. Lynn Staley, trans. and ed., *The Book of Margery Kempe* (New York: W. W. Norton & Company, 2001), 16, 37.

6. Quoted by Clarissa W. Atkinson, "Female Sanctity in the Late Middle Ages," in ibid., 228.

7. Hildegard of Bingen, Letter in Introduction to *Scivias*, trans. by Columba Hart and Jane Bishop (New York: Paulist Press, 1990), cited by Flinders, *A Little Book of Women Mystics*, 19.

8. Julian of Norwich, *Revelations of Divine Love*, chapter 86, found

on http://home.infionline.net/~ddisse/julian.html.

9. Staley, *The Book of Margery Kempe*, 16, 21.

10. Mechthild of Magdeburg, quoted in, "Other Women's Voices," http://home.infionline.net/~ddisse/mechthil.html.

11. Carmen Acevedo Butcher, compiler, *Incandescence: 365 Readings with Women Mystics* (Orleans, MA: Paraclete Press, 2005), 70.

SUGGESTIONS FOR FURTHER READING

THE MIDDLE AGES

Amt, Emilie, *Women's Lives in Medieval Europe: A Sourcebook* (New York: Routledge, Chapman and Hall, Inc., 1993)

Bitel, Lisa M., *Women in Early Medieval Europe* (New York: Cambridge University Press, 2002)

Bynum, Caroline Walker, *Holy Feast and Holy Fast: The Religious Significance of Food to Medieval Women* (Berkeley, CA: University of California Press, 1987)

Bynum, Caroline Walker, *Jesus as Mother* (Berkeley, CA: University of California Press, 1982)

Bynum, Caroline Walker, *The Resurrection of the Body in Western Christianity 200–1336* (New York: Columbia University Press, 1995)

Bynum, Caroline Walker and Paul Freedman, editors, *Last Things: Death and the Apocalypse in the Middle Ages* (Philadelphia: University of Pennsylvania Press, 2000)

Cahill, Thomas. *Mysteries of the Middle Ages: The Rise of Feminism, Science, and Art from the Cults of Catholic Europe* (New York: Doubleday, 2006)

Cantor, Norman F., general editor, *The Encyclopedia of the Middle Ages* (New York: Viking, 1999)

Cherry, Steve, "Medicine and Gender," syllabus for autumn 2004 course at the University of East Anglia, England http://www.nlm.nih.gov/hmd/collections/digital/syllabi/pdf/cherry2.pdf

Dinshaw, Carolyn and David Wallace, editors, *The Cambridge Companion to Medieval Women's Writings* (New York: Cambridge University Press, 2003)

Dronke, Peter, *Women Writers of the Middle Ages* (New York: Cambridge University Press, 1984)

Eastwood, Kay, *Women and Girls in the Middle Ages* (New York: Crabtree Publishing Company, 2004)

Gies, Frances & Joseph, *Women in the Middle Ages: The Lives of Real Women in a Vibrant Age of Transition* (New York: Harper Perennial, 1978)

"The ORB: On-line Reference Book for Medieval Studies" (http://www.the-orb.net), maintained at the College of Staten Island, City University of New York

Power, Eileen, *Medieval Women* (Cambridge: Cambridge University Press, 1995)

Spearing, Elizabeth, editor, *Medieval Writings on Female Spirituality* (New York, Penguin Books, 2002)

Tanner, Norman P., *The Church in Late Medieval Norwich 1370–1532* (Studies and Texts 66. Toronto: Pontifical Institute of Mediaeval Studies, 1984)

Vass, Deborah, "The World Civilization Virtual Library. Georgia College & State University. Milledgeville, Georgia, http://www.faculty.de.gcsu.edu/~dvess/ids/fap/hildegard.htm

Ward, Jennifer, *Women in Medieval Europe 1200–1500* (Edinburgh: Longman, 2002)

White, Hugh, Translator, *The English Text of the Ancrene Riwle* (London: Oxford University Press, 1972)

MEDIEVAL MYSTICS

Armstrong, Regis J., editor and translator, *Clare of Assisi: Early Documents* (New York: Paulist Press, 1988)

Atherton, Mark, *Hildegard of Bingen: Selected Writings* (London: Penguin Classics, 2001)

Butcher, Carmen Acevedo, *Incandescence: 365 Readings with Women Mystics* (Orleans, MA: Paraclete Press, 2005)

Carey, Grant S., "A Visit with Margery Kemp," Trinity Cathedral, Sacramento, California http://www.trinitycathedral.org/ccckempe.html

Crampton, Georgia Ronan, "*The Shewings of Julian of Norwich*: Introduction," http://www.lib.rochester.edu/camelot/julianin.htm#f7, Kalamazoo, Michigan: Medieval Institute Publications, 1994

Crawley, David, "The Green-Fingered God," *Reality Magazine*, volume 52, published by the Bible College of New Zealand

Disse, Dorothy, webmaster, "Other Women's Voices: Women's Writing Before 1700," http://home.infionline.net

Dorman, Marianne, "The Beguines," http://mariannedorman.home-stead.com/Beguines.html

Flinders, Carol Lee, *Living Portraits of Seven Women Mystics* (New York: HarperCollins, 1993)

Flinders, Carol Lee, editor, *A Little Book of Women Mystics* (New York: HarperSanFrancisco, 1995)

Furlong, Monica, compiler, *Visions and Longings: Medieval Women Mystics* (Boston: Shambhala, 1997)

Furlong, Monica, *The Wisdom of Julian of Norwich* (Grand Rapids, MI: William B. Eerdmans Publishing Company, 1996)

Frank, Tobin, *Mechthild von Magdeburg: The Flaming Light of the Godhead* (New York: Paulist Press, 1992)

Hart, Mother Columba, editor and translator, *Hadewijch: The Complete Works* (New York: Paulist Press, 1980)

Holloway, Julian Bolton, "The Cell of Self-Knowledge: The Soul Within," http://www.umilta.net/cell.html

Hozeki, Bruce W., editor and translator, *The Book of the Rewards of Life* by Hildegard of Bingen (New York: Oxford University Press, 1997)

Kavanaugh, Kieran and Otilio Rodriguez, translators, *The Collected Works of St. Teresa of Avila* (Washington, DC: Institute Carmelite Studies, 1980)

King, Ursula, *Christian Mystics: The Spiritual Heart of the Christian Tradition* (New York: Simon & Schuster, 1998)

King, Ursula, *Christian Mystics: Their Lives and Legacies throughout the Ages* (Mahwah, NJ: HiddenSpring, 2001)

Kirvan, John, *Let Nothing Disturb You: A Journey to the Center of the Soul with Teresa of Avila* (Notre Dame, Indiana: Ave Maria Press, 2001)

Law, Sarah, "'A Room of Her Own' Julian, Prayer and Creativity," 2003 Annual Julian Lecture, St. Julian's Church, Norwich, England, May 3, 2003

Noffke, Suzanne, translator, *Catherine of Siena: The Dialogue* (Paulist Press, 1980)

Paschal, Gehres, "12th Century Medical Treatments Described in Hildegard's Cause et Cure and the Success of 21st Century Pharmaceutical and Medical Research," found at www.uga.edu/juro/2004/paschal.htm

Pawlik, Manfred, Patrick Madigan, Mary Palmquist and John Kulas, translators and editors, *Holistic Healing* by Hildegard of Bingen (Collegeville, MN: Liturgical Press, 1994)

Petroff, Elizabeth A., *Body and Soul: Essays on Medieval Women and Mysticism* (New York: Oxford University Press, 1995)

Petroff, Elizabeth Alvilda, editor, *Medieval Women's Visionary Literature* (New York: Oxford University Press, 1986)

Schmitt, Miriam & Linda Kulzer, editors, *Medieval Women Monastics: Wisdom's Wellsprings* (Collegeville, MN: Liturgical Press, 1996)

Staley, Lynn, translator and editor, *The Book of Margery Kempe* (New York: W.W. Norton & Company, 2001)

Strehlow, Wighard, *Hildegard of Bingen's Spiritual Remedies* (Rochester, VT: Healing Arts Press, 2002)

Underhill, Evelyn. *Mysticism* (First published in 1911, now available online at http://www.ccel.org/ccel/underhill/mysticism.html)

Upjohn, Sheila, *Why Julian Now? A Voyage of Discovery* (Grand Rapids, MI: William B. Eerdmans Publishing Co., 1997)

van den Dungen, Wim, translator, *On Seven Ways of Holy Love by Beatrice of Nazareth*, http://www.sofiatopia.org/equiaeon/7ways.html

Wolters, Clifton, translator, *Revelations of Divine Love* by Julian of Norwich (London: Penguin Classics, 1966)

MODERN MIDLIFE

Cooper, Sue Ellen, *The Red Hat Society: Fun and Friendship After Fifty* (New York: Warner Books, 2004)

Crafton, Barbara Cawthorne, "Rematch: The Old Enemies," June 7, 2004 The *Almost* Daily eMo, http://www.geraniumfarm.org/dailyemo.cfm?Emo=274

Crafton, Barbara Cawthorne, "Jesus Claims Some Quiet Time," February 1, 2006 The *Almost* Daily eMo http://www.geranium-farm. org/dailyemo.cfm?Emo=604

Haddon, Dayle, *The Five Principles of Ageless Living* (New York: Atria Books, 2003)

Hamilton, Joan, "Woman of the Year," *Town & Country* magazine, January, 2006

Hubert, Cynthia, "Best friends: When it comes to relationships, there's no match for the bond between women," *Sacramento* (CA) *Bee*, March 5, 2006, Scene Section, page L1

Hunter, Ski, Sundel, Sandra S., Sundel, Martin, *Women at Midlife: Life Experience and Implications for the Helping Professions.* Washington, DC: National Association of Social Workers, 2002

Ko, Daniel, "Religious Coping Plays a Role in Recovery From Depression," http://www.mental-health-today.com/articles/spirituality.htm

Marcel, Joyce, "I'm an Old Woman, Hear Me Roar," *The American Reporter Vol. 12, No. 2861–March 27, 2006*

The New York Times, Women's Health Special Edition, June 21, 1998, http://www.nytimes.com/specials/women/whome/ depression.html

Northrup, Christiane, *The Wisdom of Menopause: Creating Physical and Emotional Health and Healing During the Change* (New York: Bantam Books, 2001)

Shellenbarger, Sue, *The Breaking Point! How Female Midlife Crisis is Transforming Today's Women* (New York: Henry Holt, 2004)

Tannen, Deborah, *You're Wearing That?* (New York: Random House, Inc., 2006)

Tucker-Ladd, Clayton E., *Changing Your Self-concept and Building Your Self-esteem* (Online book published by in1996 found at http://mentalhelp.net/psyhelp)

Vickers-Willis, Robyn, *Navigating Midlife: Women Becoming Themselves* (New South Wales: Allen & Unwin, 2002)

Judith Viorst, *Grown-Up Marriage: What We Know, Wish We Had Known, and Still Need to Know About Being Married* (New York:

Free Press, 2004)

Woolf, Virginia, *A Room of One's Own* (New York: Harcourt, Inc, 1989)